echoes
among the stars

echoes

among the stars

A SHORT HISTORY OF THE U.S. SPACE PROGRAM

Patrick J. Walsh

M.E.Sharpe
Armonk, New York
London, England

Library of Congress Cataloging-in-Publication Data

Walsh, Patrick J., 1963–
    Echoes among the stars : a short history of the U.S. space program
/   Patrick J. Walsh.
          p.   cm.
    Includes bibliographical references and index.
    ISBN 0-7656-0537-6 (alk. paper)
    ISBN 0-7656-0538-4 (pbk. alk paper)
    1. Astronautics—United States—History. I. Title
TL789.8.U5W3   2000
629.4′0973—dc21   99-38899
                                                                          CIP

Printed in the United States of America

The paper used in this publication meets the minimum requirements of
American National Standard for Information Sciences
Permanence of Paper for Printed Library Materials,
ANSI Z 39.48-1984.

BM (c)   10   9   8   7   6   5   4   3   2
BM (p)   10   9   8   7   6   5   4   3   2   1

I dedicate this work to my parents, whose faith has never wavered.

Table of Contents

Acknowledgments

This work could not have been imagined, let alone completed, without enormous amounts of inspiration, support, and love. For all their help over a very long period of time, I would like to acknowledge the encouragement of my parents, John E. and Helen E. Walsh, my brother, Michael, my sister-in-law, Eneida, and my niece and nephews, Kelliann, Michael, and James. My aunt, Sister Margaret Walsh, must also be singled out for the special support she has given this project. Anyone who has felt the warmth of a supportive family will surely understand my enduring gratitude for those who are closest to my life and work.

I have also had the good fortune of easy access to a number of close business associates and friends who are always receptive to discussions about my ideas and the progress of my research and writing. For the remarkably open and productive environment these special people have helped to create for me over the past decade, I offer heartfelt thanks to Alex Mendelsohn, a superb editor and loyal friend, and to Steven Borzoni and Margie Burns, for their generous professional and personal support of this project in particular, and of my career in general.

In addition, I would also like to thank all those who read various portions of my "space book" manuscript in various stages of its progress and who lent their enthusiasm to the work and its author. Suze Albright Lewitt, Dave Lewitt, Lennox Holness, Marshall and Cecilia Woodall, and Jen Brennan have been particularly kind in this respect.

There have also been a large number of academic supporters and friends who have encouraged my research and writing, foremost among them Dr. Lawson Bowling, Sister Ruth Dowd, Dr. Ruth Eisenberg, Professor John S. Joy, Professor Robert Klaeger, Dr. Howard Livingston, Dr. Charles Masiello, and Dr. Donald Ryan.

Finally, I wish to acknowledge all those who have believed in this project, inquiring about its progress and direction and offering encouragement along the way. Many of these supporters have been my students at Pace University; the love for the future expressed by them and their counterparts at colleges and high schools across the country was a renewing inspiration throughout the process of completing this project.

echoes

among the stars

1

NASA Lifts Off: The 1950s

The story of how humanity first managed to break free of its cradle, earth, and venture into the vastness of space begins, appropriately enough, with an international conference. Convened in Rome in October of 1954 to plan the International Geophysical Year of 1957–1958, the gathering of scientists from forty different countries resulted in a far-ranging plan of experiments and exploration in disciplines as varied as physics, geology, meteorology, and aerospace. Of all the ambitious objectives the participants sought to undertake, the most novel was the plan to launch a small satellite into earth orbit.

A modest goal by modern standards, the plan to send a basketball-sized probe containing few (if any) scientific instruments into orbit around the earth seemed a fantastic notion to the average American when it was formally introduced in July 1955. As a result of the Rome conference and in cooperation with other countries, the U.S. government announced its intent to play the leading role in the satellite launch.

Following a familiar pattern, the government of the Soviet Union also announced a plan to send a satellite into orbit during the International Geophysical Year.[1]

The American move was both strategic and tactical, and its aims were political as well as scientific. Far beyond the obvious benefits to space science that would result from the development of the equipment, systems, and procedures necessary to create and launch the satellite, the U.S. effort was also calculated as a means to outpace the USSR's increasingly optimistic pronouncements about the progress of its own space plans. Thus the seeds of the space race, as it would become known in earnest within the next decade, were sown in the mid-1950s.

Spoils of War, Visions of Space

For both the United States and the USSR, the first fruits of the Allied victory in World War II included a generous portion of German rocket technology, as well as many of the scientists and technicians who had developed it. Of particular interest to both sides was the German V-2 rocket; many of the Soviets' earliest steps toward space were based on further development of the basic V-2, and the United States began firing captured V-2s as well as American-made counterparts in White Sands, New Mexico, in 1946.

The Soviets incorporated many German technicians into their rocket development efforts immediately after the war, gaining the benefit of their expertise and then gradually allowing them to return to Germany in the early 1950s. But, fearing Soviet retribution for Hitler's savage Russian campaigns, a large majority of the most sought-after German scientists surrendered to the Western Allies at the end of the war. As a result, the United States received the lion's share of V-2 rocket expertise, including the skills of pioneering space scientists Hermann Oberth and Wernher von Braun.[2]

Given the political and social climate of the day, with the former allies sliding precariously into the first decade of the nuclear age and the initial years of the cold war, it seems inevitable—and in many ways beneficial—that the United States and USSR would embark on a decade-long competition to send first satellites, then human beings, into orbit and eventually to the moon. The two nations' race to develop their space programs coincided with the initial stage of their harrowing development of vast stockpiles of nuclear weapons. Locked into an arms race that by its nature provided no hope of victory but at the same time gave neither side any practical way to withdraw, America and the Soviet Union feverishly pursued the benefits of propaganda and prestige that early hegemony in space could provide.

From the beginning, the contest of technologies and engineering skills reflected the central tenets of each nation's belief system. Superiority in the space race was increasingly seen as a validation of national pride and the preeminence of one way of life over the other. And even as the cold war ground on, with its intransigent nuclear adversaries a world apart in ideology as well as geography, humanity's shared preoccupation with space offered a proving ground for the first great superpowers that reduced their potential for fatal miscalculation more than any comparable earthbound alternative.[3]

First Sounds from Space: *Sputnik 1*

On October 4, 1957, 10:28 p.m. Moscow time, the USSR launched the *Sputnik 1* satellite from a site in Tyuratam, in Soviet Central Asia. A simple device, an aluminum sphere with four antennas and a radio transmitter, *Sputnik 1* was the first human-made object to orbit the earth. The space age had begun.

The tiny satellite, weighing in at just under 185 pounds, its radio transmitting an innocuous beep that ham radio operators around the world could hear as it passed overhead, had an immediate galvanizing effect on American popular opinion. That the Soviets had beaten the Americans into space was bad enough, but many Americans worried about the achievement's larger implications for the magnitude of the Soviet military threat; to a large degree, the idealism of space exploration and the fear of powerful rocket-mounted weaponry went hand in hand in the early years.[4] Members of Congress and various media representatives wondered aloud whether rockets powerful enough to send radios into space would also be powerful enough to send nuclear warheads careening toward American cities, and worried openly about the national-security threat the satellite posed for the United States and Western Europe, as it passed overhead every hour and a half.[5] Such fears were exacerbated by Soviet leader Nikita Khrushchev, who consistently politicized the achievements of *Sputnik 1* and its successors to promote Soviet ideology around the globe and consolidate his own political power at home.[6]

U.S. president Dwight Eisenhower, meanwhile, sought to downplay the military significance of *Sputnik 1*. In several major speeches, he reassured the American people that the Soviet space probe presented no practical military threat, and he repeatedly stated that he was confident that an American satellite would soon be joining *Sputnik 1* in the heavens. Eisenhower is often represented as having underestimated the importance of the Soviets' fast start in space, but the gradual declassification of documents from the early cold-war era indicate otherwise. Details of the Naval Research Laboratory's Galactic Radiation and Background (GRAB) satellite, for example, demonstrate the president's clear understanding of the intelligence benefits of the early space program.[7]

Design work on the GRAB satellite began within a year of the first Sputnik flight, and the odd-shaped ball—looking much like an old-fashioned deep-sea diver's helmet with too many view holes—was launched on June 22, 1960. The launch took place just five days after U.S. pilot Francis Gary Powers was shot down by the Soviets in his U-2 spy plane. Powers's capture led to an embarrassing public disclosure of American spying techniques, and added a bit of tarnish to Eisenhower's considerable reputation as an exceptional commander in chief. Only a small handful of government officials were aware at the time that the country's spying efforts were already advancing into space, a fact that, had it been disclosed, might well have laid to rest a good deal of public anxiety about the so-called missile gap between the United States and USSR.[8]

The president's insistence that the United States was not far behind the Soviets generally fell on deaf ears in Congress and the media, and the issue grew in stature during the 1960 presidential campaign between Eisenhower's vice president, Richard M. Nixon, and Democratic challenger John F. Kennedy.

Well Ahead of Sputnik: Early U.S. Satellite Surveillance

In retrospect, it is obvious that Eisenhower understood the need for American space successes that could be made public. At the same time, he was also aware that such a program would be a long, arduous undertaking that would require years of hard work before the United States could surpass the Soviets. The secret spy satellite, on the other hand, was immediately useful in the short term for detecting Russian air defenses, and arguably put the United States well ahead of the Soviets in the burgeoning space race. In fact, the only major drawback of the tiny GRAB device was that the government couldn't tell anyone about it. (The satellite's existence was made public by the Naval Research Lab and the National Reconnaissance Office in June 1998, in honor of the navy lab's seventy-fifth anniversary).[9]

While the U.S. program raced to catch up, the Soviets enjoyed further success with the launch of *Sputnik 2* on November 3, 1957. In this second satellite, a much larger, heavier craft, the Soviets included a female husky named Laika, who enjoyed a "dog's-eye view" of the earth from space. The craft's pressurized cabin and life-support system represented a remarkable achievement in systems engineering, and the project garnered valuable biomedical data for a week before life support ran out and the dog was put to sleep.

The American path into space featured several roads being traveled all at once, with separate systems being developed by the Naval Research Laboratory, the army, and the air force. The navy's Vanguard program got the initial go-ahead, but lost its chance to put the first U.S. satellite into orbit with an early-December failure of its three-stage test vehicle.

The launch of *Explorer 1* on January 31, 1958, led the way into space for the United States. The tiny satellite lifted off atop a modified Jupiter rocket developed in large part from the blueprint of the German V-2 and the expertise of Wernher von Braun. While primarily remembered for redeeming America's virtue in light of the achievements of the first two Sputniks, *Explorer 1* also demonstrated the practical scientific value of space exploration, as it discovered the earth's radiation belts, later named for Dr. James Van Allen, who had the foresight to equip the tiny satellite with a Geiger counter. Khrushchev ridiculed *Explorer 1* for its small size, but made no mention of a subsequent Soviet failure the following month.[10]

The Vanguard program redeemed itself handsomely in March of that same year, lifting *Vanguard 1* into an orbit that it maintains to this day. In fact, *Vanguard 1* is expected to remain in orbit for the next 250 years or so, until sometime around 2250.[11]

Space science took another leap forward with the Soviet launch of *Sputnik 3* on May 15, 1958. The satellite's mini-laboratory transmitted data about the earth's ionosphere, magnetic field, radiation belts, and cosmic rays for nearly two years.

Dancing With the Moon: *Luna 3*

The final stages of the first era of space exploration pointed explicitly toward the future. The Soviets began aiming unmanned probes at the moon in the fall of 1958, and flew past it with the *Luna 1* probe in January 1959. *Luna 1* continued on into solar orbit, accomplishing yet another first. *Luna 2* was launched September 12, 1959, and completed its mission two days later, when it crash-landed in Mare Imbrium on the surface of the moon. And on October 4—the second anniversary of the *Sputnik 1* launch—*Luna 3* lifted off. Three days later it solved one of humanity's most enduring cosmographical mysteries when it captured the first photographic images of the moon's far side.[12]

U.S. attempts to equal the Soviet moon accomplishments were hindered by a series of failed launches in 1958 and 1959. In March of 1959 the American Pioneer satellite shot past the moon and into orbit around the sun, as *Luna 1* had a few months earlier. Three more American lunar probes failed even to reach earth orbit between November 1959 and the end of 1960, and American attempts to reach the moon then ended until the advent of the Lunar Orbiter, Ranger, and Surveyor projects of the mid-1960s.

The main accomplishments of the U.S. program in the late 1950s were more organizational than operational. Acutely aware of the need to appropriately separate civilian and military authority based on his own experiences as supreme commander of Allied forces in World War II, President Eisenhower suggested to Congress in April 1958 that the U.S. space program be placed under civilian control. Given the climate of the time, with Americans' fear running rampant in response to the tensions generated by the arms race, the cold war, and the USSR's Sputnik successes, it was a courageous decision.[13]

Congress agreed that the exploration and potential development of space should be governed by civilian rather than military authority, and as a result, the National Aeronautics and Space Administration (NASA) was formed on October 1, 1958, with T. Keith Glennan as its first administrator. NASA absorbed the former National Advisory Committee for Aeronautics, which had been established in 1915, and assumed complete responsibility for America's space program, except for those activities necessary for national defense, which would remain the responsibility of the military.

Eisenhower's foresight effectively ended the interservice squabbling that characterized the attempts to launch the first U.S. satellite, and opened the space agency to a wider array of engineering and scientific talent. Perhaps most important of all, it established an aura of civilian participation that would seem in later years to give average Americans a stake in the program's success or failure. The connection between the support of the general public and the agency's ability to receive and maintain the funding necessary for its eventual trip to the moon was fundamental from the very beginning.[14]

The wide involvement of ordinary citizens also spoke to the basic American ideal of honest and open government. Inherent in NASA's role as America's civilian space authority is the promise that at each step along the way, in success or failure, the agency will be accountable to the American people.

Soviet Intransigence: The "Chief Designer"

In stark contrast, the Soviet program was tightly controlled by the central authority of the Communist government. Few details of flights, payloads, or the success or failure of a mission's objectives were ever released until a flight had been deemed a success.

The career of Sergei Korolev offers a prime example of the space program's success in spite of the encumbrances of the Soviet political system. A visionary scientist, Korolev was involved in pioneering jet propulsion research in the 1930s when he was imprisoned as a result of Soviet leader Josef Stalin's mass purges. He emerged from prison after World War II, when Stalin sought the expertise of scientists able to assist in the development of the V-2 rocket technology captured from the Germans. Following Stalin's death in 1953, Korolev became a leading figure in the Soviet space program, and he was prominently involved until his own death in 1966.

Korolev's early contributions were immensely important to the initial success of the Soviet program. He remained focused on the important goals of space exploration despite Khrushchev's constant demands for risky, distracting "stunts" for propaganda use, and his death has often been cited as a prime reason for the Soviet program's subsequent failures.[15]

Through all the years of Korolev's early leadership and despite the magnitude of his achievements, however, the imposing security of the totalitarian system dictated that the Soviets refer to their master scientist only as the program's "chief designer of carrier rockets and spacecraft." Korolev's name was made public for the first time on the occasion of his death.[16]

The Soviet penchant for dissembling and frequently, outright lying caused many of the essential facts about the USSR's space efforts to be lost to history. Even more insidious is the deliberate misinformation that was sometimes fed to the world press as a means of covering up the program's failures or shortcomings. Despite this, a good deal of accurate information did leak out over the years, and with the breakup of the Soviet Union, a cache of previously secret material has emerged.

The difference in approach went well beyond the dissemination of names and other information, however. The fundamental differences in outlook and attitude that characterized the American and Soviet space programs from the very beginning would have a great deal to do with their eventual successes and failures. The American emphasis on civilian control and the individual skills and temperament of the astronaut, engineer, and administrator would lead to a program very different from the Soviet model, which relied heavily on centralized authority and centrally controlled systems and missions.[17]

The End of the 1950s

As the decade came to an end, so did the first phase of space exploration. The Soviets had achieved about all that their technology would allow at that time, and had exhausted the propaganda benefits of their considerable space achievements. The USSR's early lead in the space race had paid handsome earthbound benefits, especially in the growing perception that superior Soviet rocket technology had allowed them to produce more intercontinental ballistic missiles (ICBMs) than the United States. The resulting "missile gap" was nervously discussed throughout Eisenhower's final two years in office, and furiously debated during the 1960 presidential campaign.

Following the success of *Luna 3*, the Soviets attempted several launches in the early part of 1960 that failed. But the minor setbacks merely marked the end of the wildly successful first stage of the country's foray into space. The Soviets were clearly ahead of their superpower rival, and had already begun to develop new systems for the next logical step in their program: to put a human being into orbit.[18]

During the same period, the U.S. effort to keep pace with the Soviet program was hampered by the Americans' inability to develop a powerful, reliable rocket system that could consistently send even small spacecraft into orbit. The American public bristled at the maddening spectacle of successive launch failures, and grew increasingly worried about the broader implications of the seemingly unbroken string of Soviet achievements.[19]

Once the Korean War had been negotiated to a standoff early in Eisenhower's first term, the United States enjoyed a brief period of respite from active combat and a general boost in prosperity for a majority of its citizens. The American economy saw a rapid and sustained expansion throughout the late 1940s and early 1950s, and by mid-decade the country's workforce shifted officially into the postindustrial age, as white-collar workers outnumbered their blue-collar counterparts for the first time in American history.[20]

The president himself became the overriding symbol of peace and progress; as an impeccably "nonpolitical" politician, he skillfully translated his World War II leadership skills into the civilian authority of the presidency, and his confidence was reflected in the self-assurance of his constituents.

But as the decade came to a close, it was clear to most Americans that the United States was behind in the nascent field of space technology, and anxiety about the arms race, the cold war, and the Sputniks reached a peak as the nation pondered its future course at the end of Eisenhower's second and final term as president.[21]

2

Project Mercury: Setting the Sights

I believe that this nation should commit itself to achieving the goal, before this decade is out, of landing a man on the moon and returning him safely to earth. No single space project in this period will be more impressive to mankind, or more important for the long-term exploration of space; and none will be so difficult or expensive to accomplish.

—*President John F. Kennedy, special message to Congress on urgent national needs, May 25, 1961*

Few Americans, in Congress, the media, the general public, or even within NASA itself, have ever had as broad an understanding of the importance of space exploration to the daily activities of the nation as President Kennedy. He championed the space effort as an idealistic, noble endeavor of human adventure, with its wisdom self-evident, its necessity self-sustaining.[1]

He also understood the practical threat that the Soviet space advantage posed to the delicate global political landscape of the early 1960s. At the height of the cold war, struggling to convince uncommitted nations of the efficacy of their particular system of government and way of life, the United States and USSR both sought to validate their claims of technical, political, and social preeminence by developing a superior space program. But while Khrushchev used the Soviet achievements as a bludgeon, Kennedy defined the American space agenda as something larger and more important than merely an easy source of propaganda or rhetoric.

Framing the task as a great adventure on an ultimate frontier, Kennedy saw the daunting cost and required technical expertise as an opportunity to bridge some of the distances between nations here on earth. Late in 1959 he expressed his preference that the effort be "placed on an international footing as soon as possible," with U.S. allies playing a significant role; despite the climate of the times, he even publicly entertained the idea of a joint effort with the Soviets. He elegantly expressed that possibility in his 1961 inaugural address: "Let both sides seek to invoke the wonders of science instead of its terrors. Together let us explore the stars."[2] Given their leadership position, however, the Soviets had little incentive to pursue the idea. In fact, Khrushchev had vastly different plans in mind to celebrate the next great step forward in space exploration.[3]

A Face Among the Stars

That moment came on April 12, 1961, when Russian cosmonaut Yuri Gagarin lifted off at 9:07 a.m. Moscow time in his *Vostok 1* spacecraft. Radio Moscow announced the flight about an hour later, while it was still in progress, and about an hour after that, at 10:55 a.m., the flight came to an end. Gagarin safely floated back to earth on the sturdy tethers of a parachute, having ejected from the craft shortly before it landed. It was a monumental achievement. Lauded for his courage, Gagarin's easy charm belied stereotypes of the soulless Soviet technocrat. The demeanor of the handsome young cosmonaut was in sharp contrast to the more familiar image of the ham-fisted Soviet leader Khrushchev; as a result, the Russian program had an opportunity for the first time to take on a human face, to go along with its technical achievements.[4]

Space as a Mirror of Society

The United States had been first to announce its plan to send people into orbit, and had introduced its first astronauts—the "Mercury Seven"—in April 1959, more than a year before the Soviets narrowed their list of cosmonauts to the pool of six from which Gagarin was chosen. It was an odd circumstance of the times that the two programs, developed simultaneously but separately, sought and often achieved the exact same goals despite their vast differences in philosophy and technical approach.

The Russian idea was that the pilot was largely a passenger in a craft that would be controlled primarily by automated systems. A cosmonaut would be allowed to take over a craft manually only if he was suddenly faced with a drastic system failure; thus the initial cosmonauts did not have the test pilot background of their American counterparts. During Gagarin's epoch-making flight, the manual controls of his craft were disabled, to be sprung into action if and when necessary by use of a three-digit code the pilot carried in a sealed envelope.

The reliance on automation and earthbound controllers provided a certain bulwark against the potentially adverse effects of zero gravity, or in the case of a pilot's injury or illness. But whatever the advantages or disadvantages of this systems-centric method, it was at the heart of Soviet space theory throughout the program's formative years. It may well have hindered the program's progress, as a more individualistic approach would have provided valuable feedback.[5]

The American approach heavily favored the skills of the former test pilots. One of the primary guidelines for Project Mercury mandated the astronaut's ability to control the spacecraft's attitude manually, and the pilot-centric scheme remains a key precept of the U.S. program to the current day. American spacecraft employed redundant automatic systems similar to their Russian counterparts, but the astronaut was always seen as playing a larger role in guiding the craft and the mission as a whole. A number of near-misses over the years, in which quick-thinking crew members avoided potentially tragic mishaps, proved the fundamental soundness of relying so heavily on the skills of the individuals involved.

The American choice was a philosophical consideration as well as a practical one. In addition to their technical knowledge and informed judgment in crucial situations, the astronauts were also called upon to express the emotional and psychological elements of their experience, in the hope that their insights about traveling beyond the atmosphere would broaden public knowledge about space. In theory at least, a better-informed public could more rationally decide the future of the nation's space agenda.[6]

Another key difference between the U.S. and Soviet programs involved the method of landing returning spacecraft. The Russians favored a return to land, while the American engineers specifying the Mercury capsule were instructed to make the craft "satisfy the requirements for a water landing." Both methods presented a high degree of risk, and both led to frightening moments for some of the earliest space travelers.

The landing question also led the Soviet government to order Gagarin to misrepresent the details of his return to earth. Prior to the start of the space program, aircraft flight records were considered valid only if the pilot landed with the craft. The Russian government feared that Gagarin's parachute landing would lessen the impact of his achievement, perhaps even leading the West to disavow his flight, so they had him omit all reference to it in accounts of the mission. Of course, they were playing by old rules; flying in the sky and flying past it into space were two different things, and as the superpower space race began to accelerate, the world was happy to concede the difference.[7]

The interdependence of events above the earth and on its surface was at the heart of the early years of the space race. In 1961, with the Soviets well ahead, Khrushchev relentlessly drove Korolev and the Russian aerospace engineers for increasingly ambitious firsts in space. And he used each new success as part of an overall effort to further the Soviet Union's earthbound military and political ambitions.[8]

Gagarin's flight on April 12 was followed a week later by Fidel Castro's victory over U.S.-supported Cuban exiles at the Bay of Pigs. A major foreign-policy failure on all counts, the Bay of Pigs further imperiled U.S. claims of global superiority over the USSR and its Communist satellite nations.

The Mercury Idea

It was against this backdrop of global misadventure and tense superpower posturing that the first manned U.S. space program, Project Mercury, achieved its initial success. Mercury had been given life back in 1958, with three objectives: to orbit a manned spacecraft around earth; to investigate human beings' ability to function in space; and to safely recover the astronaut and spacecraft with which it would accomplish the first two goals.[9]

Mercury's success would depend on the massive deployment of technology, equipment, and industrial manufacturing capability, as well as a small group of individuals who would become America's first astronauts—and in the process, certified American heroes.

The First Astronauts

The Mercury Seven were introduced to the public by NASA administrator T. Keith Glennan on April 9, 1959. At age thirty-six, John H. Glenn Jr., a U.S. Marine Corps lieutenant colonel, was the oldest of the seven, and the senior astronaut in terms of rank. He also was the only Marine of the group. Lieutenant Commanders Walter M. "Wally" Schirra Jr. and Alan B. Shepard Jr. and Lieutenant Malcolm Scott Carpenter represented the U.S. Navy, and Captains Donald Kent "Deke" Slayton, Leroy Gordon Cooper Jr., and Virgil I. "Gus" Grissom were assigned to NASA by the U.S. Air Force.

They were all experienced test pilots with distinguished service records, and had survived an intensive five-part battery of physical and psychological tests prior to their selection. Intelligent, personable, and patriotic, the first astronauts were also independent and strong-willed. They shared an esprit de corps even more intense than the legendary empathetic loyalties of test pilots, and their common respect and admiration would grow in the coming years. The public and the media embraced them immediately as heroic figures destined to redeem America's flagging pride in the race with the Soviets.

Before they had even flown once, the astronauts were catapulted in the public imagination to a level of celebrity equal to that of famous athletes and movie stars. Like a brilliant quarterback marching down the field in the final minutes of a football game that had seemed lost, they offered hope for catching up in the space race in the short term, and a future whose excitement surpassed all previous ideas of exploration and discovery. Even the most elaborate details of the most fantastic legends, tall tales, and storybooks paled in comparison with the audacity of what the seven pleasant-looking young astronauts were now publicly committed to doing sometime within the next few years. The fact that they had not yet begun their mission mattered little to the public or the press; the optimism of the times made it easy to believe in the idea of space travel, even if its actuality was still a bit farther off in the future.[10]

Everything about the Mercury Seven seemed larger than life. In response to the public's fascination with the men and their work, a $500,000 contract with *Life* magazine was negotiated on their behalf, securing the rights to their personal accounts of life in the astronaut corps. Critics painted the agreement as a financial windfall, and questioned the propriety of the astronauts receiving payment for reporting their experiences in a taxpayer-funded government program. The public didn't seem to mind at all, however, and the amount actually paid to each of the original astronauts over the course of the Mercury program was about $71,000. As the space program expanded, a second contract was negotiated in 1963 for $1,040,000, but it turned out to be even less lucrative for each individual, as the money was divided among all the members of the first three groups of astronauts. As a result, each man received a total of about $16,250 over the next four years.[11]

Within the program, during the two years between their introduction and the day the first manned Mercury capsule lifted off, the astronauts' role became increasingly clear. Seizing the opportunity to utilize their pilots' skills and experience, NASA assigned each of them to a particular aspect of the developing Mercury system, and integrated their feedback into the design process.[12]

And while the astronauts trained and ran through elaborate simulations of their future missions, the public's fascination with them grew, spurred on by growing evidence that the last remaining obstacles to humanity's long reach toward space were gradually falling away.

America's intense fascination with the astronauts unleashed a flood of space-related products that was still flowing strongly four decades later. Space toys and games and collectibles ranged from legitimately educational items such as science kits and models of the spacecraft to those that were merely fun, including dolls and "outer space" balls.

Demand for space-themed items was particularly strong in the early years, and marketers were quick to realize the appeal. A vintage comic book advertisement from the era offers a typical example: its breathless description of the "Orbitop," a small plastic ball enclosing two tiny astronaut figures "dressed in authentic space travel outfits," promises hours of fun for children willing to buy the $1 (postpaid) "satellite on a string."

As pop culture matured along with the space effort over the years, the difference was reflected in the products. When the Mattel toy company produced a collectible set of Hot Wheels toys to commemorate John Glenn's 1998 return to space, the miniature die-cast Mercury capsule and space shuttle were accompanied by three tiny figures of the astronaut. In addition to predictable depictions of the astronaut in his silvery 1960s Mercury suit and the orange flight gear he would wear during the shuttle flight, the third figure presented the beloved space hero in a business suit, carrying a briefcase, in tribute to his four terms as a member of the U.S. Senate.

Mercury Rising

The pace of test launches increased from the summer of 1959 on, and January and February of 1961 saw two successful test flights, the first of which launched a chimpanzee, "Ham," in a suborbital trip that roughly matched the expected profile of the first manned flight.

Further evidence of the nearness of the first American venture in space was the massive NASA infrastructure that was rapidly being put into place. One of Mercury's most substantial contributions to the program's future efforts was the international communications network it necessitated for tracking the capsules and maintaining contact with the astronauts.

Balancing universal pressure to begin flights as quickly as possible with safety and scientific concerns, as well as the long-term adaptability of the lessons of Mercury to later, even more ambitious projects, NASA decided to use existing technology and equipment as much as possible, and to take the simplest available approach to designing the complex systems necessary for space travel. It was a mix that proved spectacularly successful throughout the life of the program and beyond.[13]

In January 1959, the McDonnell Aircraft Corporation won the contract to build twenty space capsules for the Mercury program. A whole new image for Americans accustomed to thinking of a spacecraft as a cylindrical flying-saucer type object, the Mercury capsule was cone-shaped, tapering to a small round cylinder at its uppermost point. The craft's rounded bottom end was covered by an ablative heat shield, designed to deflect the 3,000–degree heat of reentry into the earth's atmosphere by partially evaporating. The retro-rockets that would propel the craft out of orbit at mission's end were also attached to its wide blunt end.

Although the emphasis on technology reuse specified that existing missiles be used as launch vehicles, a great deal of thought went into the safety precautions suddenly made necessary by the prospect of setting a capsule containing a human being on top of the explosive rockets needed to propel the craft past the earth's atmosphere.[14] Redstone rockets were used for the first two Mercury missions, which were suborbital flights, and Atlas launchers were used for the program's four orbital missions. Modifications to the Atlas included the addition of an early-warning system to alert controllers of an impending failure of the launch vehicle, and a nineteen-foot escape tower was attached to the top of the capsule to pull the capsule and crew away from the massive launch rocket in the event of an emergency.

On the inside, the spaceship was an extremely snug work area for even the smallest of the original astronauts. The tiny interior space was dictated by the craft's overall dimensions: 6 feet 10 inches long by 6 feet 2½ inches in diameter.

Freedom 7: **America in Space**

Alan Shepard climbed into that tiny workspace early on the cloudy Florida morning of May 5, 1961. Each of the astronauts named the particular capsule he would fly, adding the number 7 in honor of the teamwork they shared. Shepard's choice for this first American spaceflight was *Freedom 7*, appropriate enough for the task of breaking the bonds of earth's atmosphere and aptly describing the manner in which the flight was conducted, open to the world via the mass media.

The long countdown to launch, during which the various systems and equipment necessary for the flight were carefully checked and readied, had begun at 8:30 the previous morning, with a built-in hold—NASA-speak for a planned delay—of fifteen hours kicking in when the count-down stood at six and a half hours before launch. Splitting the long process into two parts gave the huge NASA teams responsible for launch-ing the rocket and the space capsule time to rest prior to the countdown's nerve-wracking final moments.

By all accounts, the astronauts themselves seem to have been among the calmest of all those involved with the flights. By strong constitution, a sense of duty, long test pilot flight experience, or perhaps simple ac-ceptance of the magnitude of their activities, the Mercury Seven lived up to the nation's enduring interest in them and in their space exploits. Their long training and congenial temperament prepared them well for their unique mission.[15]

The countdown to the launch of *Freedom 7* resumed at 11:30 p.m. on May 4, and continued through the night; Shepard was transported to the launch pad when it reached two hours and twenty minutes before liftoff, or T minus two hours and twenty minutes. The long preparation, like the two years between the astronauts' introduction to the public and the moment of this first attempt, brought a new surge of public fascination, and a great deal of the nuts-and-bolts workings of the space program, including the arcane language of launch, flight, and recovery, became part of the American lexicon.

The fits and starts of the launch sequence only served to heighten the suspense of the endeavor, the well-paced drama of getting Shepard to the launch pad, into the capsule, and then into space merely emphasizing the heroic nature of the task. And despite all the preparation—the hours the astronaut had spent practicing every detail of his mission in simulators; the trial runs provided by past test launches; and all available data, including the fact of Yuri Gagarin's recent successful flight, indicating that space flight could be accomplished without undue physical or psychological stress on the human being in the small metal pod— no one could really know what would happen once the huge Redstone rocketed past the low clouds.[16]

The emphasis on the Russian's initial successes and the United States' need to "catch up" did nothing to lessen the sheer human adventure of both programs' earliest days. There had been some thought of readying Shepard's *Freedom 7* for an early April launch, giving rise to the possibility of beating the Soviets into space, and a final test launch of the Redstone took place on March 24. But the emphasis on safety and careful preparation was deemed more important than a headlong rush to compete with the more advanced Soviets, so the honor of being first in space went to Gagarin.

In retrospect, and given the magnitude of the accomplishments of both American and Russian space travelers throughout the 1960s and during the decades since, the space race seems a quaint antique at best, and at worst a dangerous incursion of geopolitics on science and human exploration. But the political agenda fed the public's interest and gave both nations' programs a higher profile and priority than they would have had if they had been seen as purely altruistic endeavors. Defining the high human aspirations of celestial exploration in terms of industrial and ideological competition allowed each nation to focus vast resources on the peaceful application of their technology.[17]

Once Alan Shepard had entered his Mercury capsule, the countdown started up again, and ran almost continuously until T minus fifteen minutes. The trip was really on now; fifteen minutes is close enough to actually see the planned sequence of events in the mind's eye even for those who had not run through it thousands of times already, as Shepard and all those associated with the launch had.

But during preparations for a space flight, the passing of fifteen minutes prior to a launch often takes much longer on the official clock than it does on a wristwatch in real time. At T minus fifteen minutes, fretting over the possibility that the historic launch and flight could not be properly photographed because of the low clouds that had been hanging over the pad all through the early morning hours, NASA officials decided to hold the countdown for about a half hour.

During the weather-related hold, a new difficulty cropped up when one of the Redstone's power inverters developed regulation problems. The countdown was recycled to T minus thirty-five minutes and holding, and the inverter was replaced. Proof of the space agency's foresight in developing redundancies of systems and equipment, the entire episode with the inverter took only eighty-six minutes to resolve.

There was one last hold while the craft's real-time trajectory computer was checked a final time before launch. It was found to be in excellent working order, so the clock was set running again.

Launched Upon a New Ocean

Then, at 9:34 a.m. on May 5, 1961, *Freedom 7* lifted off atop launch vehicle MR-7—the Redstone rocket. As the huge assembly blasted into the still slightly cloudy Florida sky, it simultaneously incarnated Alan B. Shepard as the first American hero of an entirely new age and launched the nation officially on the "new ocean of space," as President Kennedy had described the bold adventure some months earlier.[18]

Shepard's grand adventure was long on significance but short in duration. In accordance with the mission's limited objectives, the entire trip of the first American in space lasted just fifteen minutes and twenty-eight seconds. But the journey accomplished all of its objectives, large and small, from slimming the space race gap with the Soviets to test-firing the retro-rockets that would be necessary to later orbital flights. *Freedom 7* flew to a height of 116 miles at its maximum, beyond earth's atmosphere into space, just short of orbit. Shepard became the first to manually steer a spacecraft—no small accomplishment for the pilot-centric American program, and a harbinger of things to come.[19]

His splashdown in the Atlantic Ocean, just off Grand Bahama Island, was as flawless as his flight, and he was quickly recovered. The short shot into space cemented the astronaut's place as the premier American space hero, and an adoring public eagerly watched his return and subsequent visit to the White House.[20]

Shepard's successful flight acted as a healing tonic for Kennedy, who continued to suffer embarrassing international setbacks. In the month following the disastrous Bay of Pigs invasion, the U.S.-supported government of South Korea was overthrown by a military coup. But with Shepard safely back on earth, the president saw in the space program a decisive means of surpassing the Soviets and securing American influence throughout the world. He would later describe his decision to champion the space effort as one of the most important of his time as president.[21]

A Vision of the Moon

Thus, with just a little over fifteen minutes' experience in space, still trailing in the competition for hegemony in the cosmos and the affections of developing nations on earth, Kennedy set the sights of the U.S. space program on the moon. On May 25 he made his famous challenge to Congress, carefully noting the obvious risks and the potential benefits of his space agenda, and warned that anything less than total commitment to the long-term goal of landing on the moon would be worse than no commitment at all. He asked Congress to approve some $148 million in increased funding for space-related work, and estimated that the total cost of $531 million for fiscal 1962 would be dwarfed by the additional expenditure of $7 billion to $9 billion over the next five years.[22]

Kennedy's ambitious proposal did not seem particularly unrealistic to NASA administrator James Webb, whom Kennedy had appointed in February to replace T. Keith Glennan. With the new president's charismatic support and the pressing need to catch up to and surpass the Soviets, Webb envisioned a valedictory moon landing in late 1968 as a fitting close to JFK's second term.[23]

In June, Kennedy and Khrushchev met face-to-face at a summit in Vienna. The topics of their informal talks included Gagarin and the space race, and Kennedy casually broached the possibility of U.S.-USSR cooperation on the moon agenda. The conversation was far more serious, however, in regard to the ongoing Berlin crisis; Khrushchev warned that the Soviets were about to sign a peace treaty with East Germany that would end Western access to Berlin.[24]

As the summer wore on, both nations sped their space efforts forward. The dictates of science and safety shaped the second U.S. mission, which was to be a near-duplicate of the first. While proving the reliability of the systems and procedures that had powered Shepard's mission, the flight of Gus Grissom's *Liberty Bell 7* was also part of NASA's plan to have each astronaut run through a suborbital flight prior to an orbital attempt. As events unfolded, the move into orbit came earlier than planned.[25]

Liberty Bell 7: Perilous Success

With the stated objective of corroborating the man-in-space concept, Grissom's Mercury mission had few significant differences from Shepard's. The capsule was virtually identical, differing only in the addition of a large window, for a better view, and an explosive hatch, to replace the mechanical locks of the *Freedom 7.* Ostensibly making the craft safer in an emergency, the hatch constituted an easy way out of the small capsule, by automatically opening a gaping hole in its side.[26]

Delayed for several days by poor weather conditions, Grissom lifted off on July 21. As was the case with the first Mercury launch, the countdown was tedious toward the end, the astronaut sitting in the cramped capsule for more than three hours before the fifteen-minute flight finally got under way. One of the few holds during the countdown involved an adjustment to a misaligned hatch bolt.

Once begun, the mission went well during the trip into space and back. As the craft plummeted toward the Atlantic, its tiny drogue parachute opened at the appropriate moment, followed by the main chute, which slowed the capsule enough for a water landing. Grissom communicated his position to the recovery ships and began checking off items on his postflight checklist. Then, inexplicably, the explosive hatch on the *Liberty Bell 7* blew, and water began rushing into the capsule. Grissom scrambled out of the rapidly filling spacecraft, swimming frantically to avoid being pulled beneath the waves along with the heavy metal capsule. Fortunately, he had splashed down close enough to the targeted landing spot for the recovery forces to find him before he drowned; but *Liberty Bell 7* was lost, sinking to the ocean floor 15,000 feet below.[27]

The incident caused a furor within NASA. Some of the engineers associated with the explosive hatch contended that it could not have blown off by itself, intimating that Grissom had somehow activated it inadvertently. NASA officials and the other astronauts staunchly defended

Grissom, and a review board eventually attributed the accident to several possible mechanical or electrical failures, none of which had to do with the astronaut.

For its part, the public drew a collective sigh of relief that Grissom had not been killed during the incident, and its hero worship of the Mercury Seven continued unabated.[28]

Soviet Advances

The rest of the summer belonged to the Soviets. Khrushchev insisted that the flight of *Vostok 2* begin earlier than planned, to coincide with the construction of the Berlin Wall. With cosmonaut Gherman Titov aboard, the *Vostok 2* flight took place on August 6. Despite severe motion sickness, Titov spent an entire day in orbit and returned safely.

His exceptional achievement was overshadowed a week later, however, when Communist East Germany began construction of the Berlin Wall. Sealing off Western access to the city, the wall was a shocking testament to the USSR's influence and ambition. And just in case the message was somehow not communicated clearly enough by the efforts of the East German troops walling off Berlin, the Soviets followed the naked aggression of the wall with several tests of massive nuclear weapons at the end of the month. By exploding weapons of twenty to one hundred megatons in the atmosphere, they explicitly linked their perceptions of technological and military superiority.[29]

While the U.S. government responded with growing alarm to the Soviets' military adventures, NASA tried to figure out some way to jump-start the space program and put an American in orbit. Plans for further suborbital flights were scrapped, and in mid-September a one-orbit unmanned flight was successful, proving the mettle of the thin-skinned Atlas intercontinental ballistic missile as an able launch vehicle for future Mercury missions. During the first two U.S. ventures into space the Redstone rocket had served its purpose well, but the more powerful—and more temperamental—Atlas was vital for orbital flight.

A successful Mercury-Atlas flight, with a chimpanzee on board, took place at the end of November. The little primate, Enos, fared relatively well during his trip around the earth and landed safely, despite a number of harrowing moments. At one point the temperature inside the capsule passed 100 degrees Fahrenheit before controllers on the ground could level it off, and the flight was shortened to two orbits.

Despite a failed test of the worldwide tracking system earlier in the month, the November 29 mission cleared the way for John Glenn to attempt the first American passage into orbit. The Atlas rocket had performed well, and the manner in which the problems with the flight were overcome gave everyone associated with the program an extra boost of confidence. And as a further comfort to all those charged with Glenn's safety as the primary goal of their mission, Enos the chimp seemed little worse for wear as a result of his odyssey, having withstood 7.6 Gs and returned with three-plus hours of weightless travel around the earth under his tiny belt.

Friendship 7: America in Orbit

Hopes of launching Glenn during the Christmas holiday were frustrated by a series of maddening delays. Mechanical problems and poor weather kept Glenn out of space for eighty-two days over nine scheduled launch dates before his *Friendship 7* finally lifted off on February 20, 1962.[30]

In a flight lasting just under five hours, Glenn narrated the sights of earth from orbit, describing sunrise, sunset, oceans, mountains, deserts, the massive pyrotechnics of thunderstorms viewed from above, and the eerie magnificence of the stars from a step closer to them. At one point he even described peculiar little "fireflies" batting around outside his capsule; during the next Mercury mission these were determined to be vapor particles expelled from the craft and frozen in the vacuum of space.[31] But their appearance was something that the seemingly endless hours of simulated flying on the ground could not have anticipated, and Glenn's fascination with them was shared by millions eavesdropping on his progress from far below.[32]

Glenn traveled around the earth three times, enjoying the view and the sensation of weightlessness as well as the task of relaying his description of the events of his journey. A difficulty soon cropped up with the spacecraft's automatic steering system, however, forcing him to focus on less pleasant aspects of his new environment. As the mission neared its completion, however, that fault came to seem almost benign, as controllers on the ground suddenly found themselves faced with an unexpected warning light.

The hazard indicator pointed to the clamp that held the heat shield in place. Warning that the clamp had somehow come loose, the flashing light left the staff at mission control with a serious dilemma. If the heat shield was in fact loose, it could fly off entirely during reentry, leaving the capsule unprotected, with disastrous results for the first American in space. And even if the shield remained attached to the craft, it could still allow extreme hot spots if it were not properly secured.

After engineers on the ground fretted through their decidedly limited alternatives, an ingenious solution emerged. Attached to the heat shield was a small group of six retro-rockets that had been fired when *Freedom 7* separated from the big Atlas launch vehicle. These spent rockets were to be jettisoned prior to the capsule's plunge into the atmosphere at mission's end; but now, as a means of keeping the heat shield affixed to the spacecraft, it was decided to leave the small pack of rockets in place, in the hope that the metal straps that kept them attached to the heat shield would also help to keep the heat shield attached to *Freedom 7*.

The effect on the descending spacecraft was spectacular, as the rockets and the straps disintegrated in a flaming hail of debris, banging along the sides of Glenn's tiny capsule during his descent. Everyone watching the flight from the ground—in mission control, aboard the recovery ships, and via the mass media—held their collective breath for nearly four and a half minutes during the communications blackout while Glenn plummeted toward the ocean.[33]

It took just twenty-one minutes for the USS *Noa* to locate *Freedom 7* and haul it and John Glenn aboard. He remained within the capsule while it was picked up, despite earlier plans to exit through its top hatch while still in the water. But after a few final tense moments, he emerged intact. He had survived the fiery ordeal of the unorthodox reentry, and would from that point forward be celebrated as a living, breathing symbol of American achievement. One hundred million Americans had watched Glenn's flight on television, and following his visit to the White House, he appeared in a ticker-tape parade in New York City, during which a crowd of four million turned out to see him in person.[34]

Following his safe return, his virtual coronation as a bona fide American hero, and the cross-country tour of his *Freedom 7* capsule, the warning signal that had almost ended John Glenn's historic flight in disaster was carefully analyzed. The result of a faulty switch, the signal was found to be false; the heat shield had been firmly clamped in place throughout the entire trip.[35]

Safety First

Despite his years of test pilot experience and the fact that he'd passed the rigorous medical exams necessary for him to become one of the

Mercury Seven astronauts, Deke Slayton was removed from active flight duty prior to the next Mercury mission, which he had been scheduled to command, because of an odd heart anomaly. The condition had been deemed non-life-threatening and had never impeded his career before, but the NASA medical hierarchy decided to err on the side of caution, and insisted that Slayton be removed. It was a fortunate turn of events for the other astronauts and their future brethren; Slayton became a powerful advocate of the astronauts' point of view as the agency's administrator primarily responsible for crew selection on future flights.[36]

Aurora 7: A New Way of Seeing

Scott Carpenter was chosen in Slayton's place. Just as Grissom had duplicated Shepard's suborbital flight, Carpenter's task was to verify John Glenn's success. His *Aurora 7* lifted off on May 24, 1962, and all went well as he took photographs and performed various scientific experiments, including a study of liquids in space. He was also able to compensate for a failure in the capsule's automatic control system, again proving the usefulness of having a trained pilot in charge of the highly automated craft.

The maneuvering consumed fuel at a higher-than-expected rate, however, and ground controllers feared that the pilot had become preoccupied or disoriented. Whatever his state of mind, he was a few seconds late in firing the retro-rockets that brought the craft out of orbit, and as a result, he missed his splashdown target in the Atlantic by some 250 miles. A tense forty-minute search ensued as recovery forces scoured the ocean. They eventually found the pilot unharmed and in good spirits, and although *Aurora 7* had taken on a great deal of water and nearly sunk, Carpenter was safely out of the capsule, floating in a rubber life raft tethered to its side.

He was pulled from the raft by helicopters from the USS *Intrepid*, and the spacecraft was carefully monitored until it could be recovered some six hours later.

Despite his harrowing ordeal, Carpenter cherished his time in space, and eloquently communicated the mystical aspects of the experience to the public. His account did much to deepen the public's appreciation of the sheer joy of spaceflight, as well as its attendant dangers, and has in the intervening years become a crucial part of the history of the program's early years. The long hours prior to his recovery also gave millions of

Americans an opportunity to ponder the realities of what was at stake in the nascent space program, and to better understand the sacrifices the astronauts were willing to make for those brief moments of exhilarating flight through the heavens.[37]

The summer of 1962 saw another Soviet success, as *Vostok 3* and *Vostok 4* were launched a day apart in August. Cosmonauts Andrian Nikolayev and Pavel Popovich piloted the two vehicles, which flew side by side in orbit until August 15, when both landed safely.

In September, NASA selected a second group of astronauts: Neil A. Armstrong, Frank Borman, Charles "Pete" Conrad Jr., James A. Lovell Jr., James A. McDivitt, Elliot M. See Jr., Thomas P. Stafford, Edward H. White II, and John W. Young.[38]

Sigma 7: **Superb in Every Way**

In October, as if in answer to the harrowing ordeals of John Glenn and Scott Carpenter, Wally Schirra provided the United States with a textbook flight in his *Sigma 7* capsule. Schirra fulfilled all the objectives of his Mercury mission, a six-orbit engineering test flight, without incident. He carefully conserved fuel during the nine-hour trip and splashed down almost exactly on target. It was a much-needed example of how spaceflight could be almost routine, and it also exemplified the best of the astronauts' quiet confidence in themselves and the systems that supported them.[39]

October also brought another kind of quiet. The Cuban missile crisis enveloped the superpowers in an eerie silence, and the world watched and waited. The Soviet Union's attempt to introduce nuclear weapons into Cuba brought the United States and the USSR to the edge of the nuclear abyss before Kennedy and Khrushchev worked out a solution that allowed the Soviets to remove the missiles without appearing to have lost the standoff.

In many ways, the missile crisis was the fever that broke the worst of the cold war tensions. The superpower competition continued for decades, frequently with stresses that threatened to put one or the other side in an untenable position that might be difficult to escape, but the nearness of all-out nuclear confrontation between the United States and the USSR seemed to push the two countries onto separate, less volatile paths. Future clashes would be less direct, and it would be easier for each side to claim some measure of victory without the necessity of putting the entire earth at risk in order to do so. The planet that seemed so peaceful from space continued to harbor enormous tension, suffering, and misery, but it would also continue to harbor life as well, even after the precarious events of October, 1962.

Faith 7: The Long Ride

The Mercury era came to a close in mid-May of 1963, with Gordon Cooper's thirty-four-hour flight in *Faith 7*. Designed to evaluate the effects of longer-duration stays in space, the mission called for twenty-two orbits, during which Cooper became the first astronaut to sleep in orbit, dozing off peacefully and on schedule. The only difficulties with the mission came toward the end, when a series of faults in the electrical system forced the commander to manually control his reentry, which, calling upon his years of jet-flying experience, Cooper did admirably.[40]

The final flight of Project Mercury only heightened the public's expectations for the future, and cemented the status of the first astronauts as American icons. Cooper's ticker-tape parade attracted at least as many well-wishers as Glenn's had a year earlier. There had always been concern about the program's costs, its relative benefits, and the safety of the astronauts, but President Kennedy's framing of the space effort as a matter of national pride and human adventure had been borne out by the first Americans in space, and the public's support of and optimism about the program's future was strong, and remained so in spite of—or perhaps because of—increasingly impressive Soviet achievements.

Woman in Space

Just a month after Cooper's *Faith 7* mission, the Soviets launched cosmonaut Valery Bykovsky in *Vostok 5*, followed two days later, on June 16, 1963, by *Vostok 6*, with Valentina Tereshkova, the first woman in space. Tereshkova had been selected for the Russian program a year earlier along with four other women, none of whom would match her achievement as the years went by. Although it was subsequently used for propaganda purposes, her flight was no mere publicity stunt; she spent three days in space, more time than all the Mercury astronauts combined.[41]

She and Bykovsky both returned safely on June 19; his five-day mission is still the longest one-man spaceflight ever.

In subsequent years, Tereshkova's achievement as the first woman in space was joined by another unique first when she married Andrian Nikolayev, who had flown in space aboard *Vostok 3*. The first couple to share the experience of flying through the cosmos, their healthy child was cited as proof that there were no lasting genetic effects caused by exposure to cosmic radiation.[42]

The idea of female space travelers was less of a revolutionary concept in the Soviet Union than in the United States. The USSR had utilized female pilots in combat during World War II, often to remarkable effect, and was therefore less conditioned to automatically reject the idea of women in space. Most important, of course, the political hierarchy wanted women in the Soviet space program so they could maximize their propaganda value.[43] But Tereshkova's flight turned out to be only a short-term anomaly in the Soviet program.

NASA did select and train more than a dozen women as potential astronaut candidates throughout the Mercury years, beginning with record-setting pilot Jerrie Cobb in 1960, but the tenor of the times dictated that flying in space would be a male-dominated activity for the majority of its first two decades; no American woman flew in space until Sally Ride's trip aboard the space shuttle in 1983.[44]

Thus there were no women among NASA's third group of astronauts, selected in October of 1963. Included in this group were Edwin E. "Buzz" Aldrin Jr., William A. Anders, Charles A. Bassett II, Alan L. Bean, Eugene A. Cernan, Roger B. Chaffee, Michael Collins, Walter Cunningham, Donn F. Eisele, Theodore C. Freeman, Richard F. Gordon Jr., Russell L. Schweickart, David R. Scott, and Clifton C. Williams Jr.[45]

Theories in Action: The United States and USSR Compete

Developed along separate but parallel paths in the United States and the Soviet Union, the first phase of humanity's vault into space came to a close with the landing of the final Vostoks. Despite their many differences in philosophy and procedure, the Americans and Russians both saw the clear necessity of moving beyond solo flights, and as each made the move toward a craft that would be piloted by a two- or three-man crew, the exhilarating first series of space adventures had run its course.

For the Soviets, there had been proud accomplishments that would be etched permanently in the history books, as well as short-term political gains that gave the Soviet Union some measure of credibility in its life-

and-death ideological struggle with the United States. For the Americans, Project Mercury had established a way of doing things that was nearly as important in its systems and spirit as the program's substantial achievements were in themselves. The idea of going to the moon had been set inexorably in motion.

The U.S. space agency later estimated that nearly two million workers were involved in some way with the Mercury project, primarily via the program's 12 major contractors, 75 major subcontractors, and 7,200 "third tier" sub-subcontractors, as well as additional vendors that were apportioned some piece of the enormous amount of work vital to the development of the program's complex systems and equipment. More than 1,300 NASA employees worked on Mercury, and about 18,000 military service and Defense Department personnel were called upon to support each individual mission.[46]

Perhaps Mercury's biggest contribution was the certainty it exhibited in the face of the long odds of hazardous missions and hazardous times. It was an optimism that all those associated with the program shared with all those who were interested in its success. The astronauts exemplified the brightness of the program's future as much as the achievements of its recent past, and shared their optimism with the young president who had been their strongest supporter all along.

U.S. commitment to the idea of Americans in space would not dim with John F. Kennedy's assassination. In fact, in its own way, his tragic end secured the space program's place far into the future, painting the long way to the moon with a noble sadness that still endures years after his passing.

3

Project Gemini: A Bridge to the Moon

Much changed in America and in the world during the two years between the early summer of 1963 and the spring of 1965, with circumstance and destiny coinciding in a startling way to alter the relationship between the United States and the USSR. John F. Kennedy had been assassinated on November 22, 1963, and was succeeded as president by Lyndon Johnson; less than a year later Nikita Khrushchev was removed from power in the Soviet Union and succeeded by Leonid Brezhnev.

For all the raucous debate between the two nations about the superiority of their governmental systems and quality of life, it was largely the power of personal charisma that had raised the space race to such a fevered pitch in the first few years of the decade. Kennedy had been the most passionate and effective proponent of the U.S. space program in his time, and his commitment is still unmatched. Khrushchev, whatever the malignancy of his motives, was vital to the Soviet program's early success, as he relentlessly pushed his interwoven scientific and political agendas. His incessant demand for space firsts to gain a propaganda advantage over the United States also crippled the program's long-term chances for success, but he was, in any case, a towering influence on the first phase of U.S.-USSR competition.[1]

The Soviets made one manned foray into space in 1964, launching *Voskhod 1* on October 12. A headlong leap into the era of flights featuring multiple-member crews, the mission was commanded by Vladimir Komarov, who was joined in the Voskhod capsule—a modified Vostok—by engineer Konstantin Feoktistov and Boris Yegorov, a doctor who conducted medical tests during the flight. The traditional call to the crew in space was their earthbound leader's last official act; Khrushchev had been removed from office by the time the craft landed. Brezhnev made his first public appearance when he greeted the cosmonauts at a ceremony in Moscow following their return.[2]

The three-man flight was another impressive Soviet first in the move toward an eventual attempt on the moon, and the change in political leadership quickly focused the Russian program after several years of internal conflict among its engineers about how the lunar effort should proceed.[3]

The Kennedy Legacy

In the United States, a lasting anguish followed the Kennedy assassination and deeply influenced the workings of the Johnson administration throughout 1964. A longtime supporter of the space program, Lyndon Johnson had predicted in a 1961 memo to Kennedy, who had made him chairman of the National Aeronautics and Space Council, that the United States would catch up to the Soviets in the space race and surpass them sometime in 1966 or 1967. As president, Johnson saw to it that his optimism proved itself out. He strongly reiterated the goal of landing on the moon by the end of the decade; he defended NASA staunchly against the ever-present arguments that space travel was too costly, too risky, or too poor an investment for the potential gain; and he was instrumental in securing continued funding for the Mercury and Apollo projects throughout his administration.[4]

But superiority in the space race and the eventual lunar landings would remain associated with Kennedy in the national consciousness. The rich symbolism and suprapartisan nature of the space program made it an object of national pride and a connection between past and future. Persistent interest in the Kennedy assassination would, in years to come, fuel a growing skepticism about the official inquiry into his death, and keep his image constantly before the public. And success in space, at least through the completion of the Apollo program, would continue to be associated with the man who had first turned America's eyes toward the moon.

The late president's influence was certainly felt on the first American space efforts following his death. Project Gemini had been announced by NASA during his presidency, in December 1961. It was managed by the new Manned Spacecraft Center in Houston, Texas—a major honor for Lyndon Johnson's home state and boon to its economy. The new control center was built on a thousand acres that the Humble Oil company donated to Rice University, with the stipulation that Rice transfer the land to NASA via a ninety-nine-year lease. The result of political and practical business decisions, the Rice connection also had a certain poignancy, for it was at Rice that John Kennedy had characterized space as a new ocean demanding vigorous exploration.[5]

Soviets First to Walk in Space

The first space explorers of 1965 were the Russians Pavel Belyayev and Alexei Leonov, who lifted off in *Voskhod 2* in March.

An unmanned test flight preceded them in February, providing the first in-orbit workout for the tools that would define their spectacular mission: an airlock, containing a space suit, that could be automatically inflated by engineers on the ground. Once the *Cosmos 57* capsule was in orbit, the test of the airlock and suit went well, clearing the way for a manned mission and the world's first extravehicular activity (EVA), during which a cosmonaut would float out of a Voskhod capsule and spacewalk in the weightless vacuum.

Sometime after the successful test, the Soviet mission controllers inadvertently sent two commands to the onboard computer at the same time, overloading the capsule's electronic brain. The simultaneous signals from earth activated the craft's self-destruct mechanism, and the unmanned Voskhod exploded in a fiery mess. Although it had not resulted in loss of life, the incident was chilling testament to the razor-thin margin of error that permeated every aspect of the space program, for everyone involved on the ground or flying through the heavens.

Dark rumors also followed the fiery end of *Cosmos 57*, and the KGB reportedly investigated the possibility that the craft had been sabotaged. But the unexpected appearance of two signals at the same moment didn't necessarily translate into double agents or intentional wrongdoing, and apparently no evidence was found of anything more serious than the usual dangers of spaceflight. In any case, despite the explosion, the threat of falling behind the United States was deemed more formidable than the menace of doppelganger saboteurs, and the Soviets pressed forward with a manned mission.[6]

As the commander, Belyayev, watched, Leonov climbed into the in-flated airlock of the *Voskhod 2* while the craft passed high above the Pacific Ocean. The capsule was above Africa when Leonov left the airlock, floating free in space, becoming for a few short minutes his own earth, a vessel of humanity in the vacuum of the cosmos, and the first-ever human satellite.

Alexei Leonov's walk in space lasted twelve minutes and nine seconds. When the time came for him to reenter the airlock, he found his spacesuit had expanded more than expected, barring his way. He struggled toward the narrow entrance to the life-sustaining passage, growing more weary with each passing instant. Ingenuity saved the day when he reduced the pressure in his suit, effectively "slimming down" enough to vault back into the airlock. The exhaustive rigors of his EVA would be repeated several times by his American counterparts during Gemini missions, until procedures were eventually worked out that made space-walking substantially less dangerous, if not exactly a stroll in the park.

Once Leonov had passed through the airlock back into *Voskhod 2*, the inflatable appendage was jettisoned. The Soviet model represented a far different approach from the Gemini EVA route, in which a hatch was opened, exposing the capsule's innards—and both astronauts—to the vacuum of space. Fortunately, both approaches proved effective.

The cosmonauts' worries did not end with Leonov's safe reentry. Problems with their highly automated spacecraft made it necessary for Belyayev to take over manual control, and their return to earth was delayed for an extra orbit. The craft's balky systems caused *Voskhod 2* to miss its landing site by nearly a thousand miles, thudding it down in a remote, snowy, heavily wooded spot far from recovery forces. A long, cold night ensued. The Voskhod's heating system had been damaged beyond repair and was no use against the frigid weather, plus the craft's electric fans were locked in working mode, with the cosmonauts unable to turn them off. Helicopters located the capsule not long after its crash landing, but it wasn't until the following day that a rescue team on the ground was able to reach the site and free the crew. Belyayev and Leonov were uncomfortable but unharmed.[7]

The Soviets' Last First

Leonov's amazing achievement had once again put the Soviets just ahead of the United States in the space race; the first Gemini mission was scheduled for the week following the return of *Voskhod 2*. The moment belonged, if not to the Soviet government, then to the Russian people. They had long suffered the cruel effects of political mania, passing through Stalin's purges and weathering Hitler's onslaught during World War II, only to emerge into new conflict with an intractable superpower enemy.

In addition to putting them ahead of the Americans, their nation's successes in space presented the Russian people with an occasion to celebrate with an almost surrealistic joy. Amidst the horror of their recent history, the image of a Russian citizen catapulting humanity into the darkness of space represented a very bright light indeed.

No one at that instant could know it, in the United States or the USSR or anywhere else on earth, but the moment of Leonov's triumph would be the high-water mark for the Soviets in the race to the moon. The competition would go on at a fervent pace throughout the remaining years of the 1960s, with each side developing the necessary technology to be first to touch the lunar surface. Even without the inspiration of a charismatic leader such as John Kennedy, the Soviets craved the honor of being first on the moon at least as much as their U.S. counterparts, at the very least as the culmination of their string of early successes.

The Soviets would not miss by much. Following Leonov's momentous EVA, they gambled all they had on their lunar program; they abandoned the outmoded Voskhod, reorganized the administration of their space program, and tightened their focus on the moon by developing a whole new breed of spacecraft: the Soyuz. All future Voskhod flights were canceled by the end of 1965.[8]

Stretching Toward the Moon: Gemini Begins

Gemini, meanwhile, represented the logical next step for the U.S. program. Project Mercury, with its tiny one-man capsule, had yielded only one mission that lasted more than a day, while a typical Apollo lunar mission, designed to send three astronauts comfortably into space and land two of them on the moon, would require its crew to be "out there" for more than a week. NASA officials realized early on that the holes in their knowledge about the effects of space travel might be filled by tragic case studies unless they quickly gained more experience in long-duration flight. Gemini would give them the chance to do so, while at the same time giving the astronauts valuable hands-on experience in the skills they'd later use during Apollo.

Thus the objectives for Project Gemini included the sending of two-man crews into space for flights of up to two weeks, to broaden the agency's understanding of the effects of weightlessness and the medical and psychological impact that a long stay in space might have on its astronauts.[9]

The new spacecraft was a classic example of evolutionary engineering, providing the astronauts with an obvious step up from the Mercury. The Gemini capsule was bigger, roomier, and more functional, but it was also designed to provide fully functional early iterations of the systems necessary to navigate, maneuver, and recover the later Apollos. The ability to rendezvous and dock with other orbiting vehicles and to maneuver the combined craft using the target vehicle's propulsion system was an explicitly stated Gemini goal, with obvious implications for the later moon missions that would require the docking and joint flight of Apollo's combined command and lunar modules.[10]

In its earliest stages, Gemini also envisioned the possibility of bringing its returning capsules down on land—an option that in retrospect seems strangely foreign to anyone who can recall the singular image of a Mercury, Gemini, or Apollo capsule splashing into the sea. Coming down on land was in fact a foreign method, the one used by the Soviets; in any case, the idea was jettisoned from the Gemini plan in 1964, although the procedures necessary for returning on land were worked on and perfected to the degree that they likely would have been successful if they had been used.[11]

Of much more enduring importance was Gemini's contributions to the art of the EVA. Through hard experience and careful study, the Gemini spacewalkers gradually learned how to properly orient themselves to do useful work while floating weightlessly in space. It was a major advance, and a necessary one.[12]

The first two Gemini missions were unmanned tests, in April 1964 and January 1965. They proved the efficacy of the Titan II missile as a launch vehicle, and gave flight controllers a chance to get some "live" experience before the manned flights. *Gemini 2* suffered the indignity of dodging Florida's hurricane season during the late summer and early fall of 1964; on the run first from Hurricane Cleo and then from Hurricane Dora, the entire Gemini capsule/Titan II launch assembly was taken apart and put into storage. Reassembled, *Gemini 2* approached its scheduled launch on December 9 free from further weather worries. Unfortunately, the Titan II's malfunction detection system indicated a loss of hydraulic pressure and shut down its engines one second after ignition, aborting the mission.

Finally, on January 19, 1965, *Gemini 2* lifted off. According to plan, it quickly completed its eighteen-minute suborbital flight into space and back, and splashed down nearly on target in the Atlantic Ocean.[13]

Gemini 3: Teamwork

Alan Shepard and Tom Stafford were initially chosen for the first manned Gemini flight. The selection procedure, headed by Shepard's sidelined Mercury Seven colleague Deke Slayton, was becoming more complex as NASA enlarged its astronaut corps, adding nine new members in 1962 and fourteen more in 1963. Shepard, of course, had been the first American in space; Stafford was a highly regarded member of the second group.

Highly competent, well respected by his peers, and already revered by the public for his first venture into space, Alan Shepard looked forward to inaugurating the manned portion of the Gemini program. But before the flight could take place, he developed an inner-ear imbalance that caused him to experience severe attacks of dizziness. As a result, he was removed from active flight status, and the backup crew of Gus Grissom and John Young was assigned to the mission.[14]

It was a setback flush with irony for Shepard and Slayton. Close friends, their past commiseration over Slayton's health problems gave Shepard's difficulties a depressing sense of déjà vu. Fortunately, neither man's condition would ultimately prove irreparable, and both Shepard and Slayton were eventually returned to active flight status. Shepard landed on the moon as commander of *Apollo 14*; Slayton flew into space as part of the crew of the Apollo-Soyuz Test Project.

The first manned moments of Gemini, however, belonged to Gus Grissom and John Young. With a whimsy that was lost on NASA administrators, Grissom dubbed the capsule *Molly Brown*, a reference to the popular Broadway play *The Unsinkable Molly Brown*. It was a subtle jibe at the Mercury capsule that had nearly caused him to drown when it disappeared beneath the waves of the Atlantic nearly four years earlier.

The agency's concern that the nickname might undercut the mission's serious intent was muted by the public's ongoing enthusiasm. Even so, the astronauts' penchant for naming their spacecraft would be reined in after the flight, until the Apollo program, when distinct names would be required to identify separate craft flying in space at the same time.[15]

As it turned out, Grissom and Young were able to validate the Gemini capsule as an advance over the Mercury design in both architecture and equipment. Lifting off atop a Titan II on March 23, 1965, they spent three orbits and nearly five hours in space. They performed several experiments that were only partially successful, due to faulty equipment (photography, for example, was hindered by an improper lens setting, and an equipment failure wrecked an experiment designed to gauge the effect of zero gravity on sea urchin eggs). Most important, they were able to maneuver the craft into higher and lower orbits—an ability of great importance to the program's future plans.

Testing the Gemini system in space for the first time, their primary objectives were the standard goals of any craft on its first occupied voyage: a safe launch, flight, and return. These were the same aims set for Alan Shepard during the Mercury program's first flight into space, and for John Glenn during the first orbital mission. And they would also be the primary ambitions of *Apollo 1* two years later.[16]

Part of the mission profile for *Gemini 3* called for it to demonstrate controlled reentry and landing techniques. Unfortunately, the craft returned at a lower-than-anticipated angle, so the procedure was only partially successful. While there was no harm to the crew, the capsule splashed down about seventy miles from its target, and it took about an hour for the USS *Intrepid* to bring Grissom and Young aboard. Despite the minor glitches along the way, though, it was a far happier finish for Gus Grissom than the last time he'd returned from space. To its credit, and the relief of an appreciative Grissom and Young, *Molly Brown* proved authentically unsinkable.

The success of their mission was probably best summed up by the minor furor that ensued afterward, over a practical joke Young had played during the flight. Goaded by Wally Schirra, Young had smuggled a corned beef sandwich on board for Grissom. The sight of the definitively earthly lunch meat in the austere, high-tech space capsule was yet another example of the astronauts' good-natured humor, endearing in retrospect, and understandable in the context of lightening the emotional weight of the task at hand. But the stunt was viewed in dire terms by NASA's nonastronaut personnel. Still unsure about the potential effects of space travel on the human body, and concerned about the impact of even the smallest unforeseen changes to the exhaustively detailed and closely monitored capsule environment, the agency set new limits on the types of personal items astronauts could carry with them on future trips.[17]

Astronaut Culture

The entire incident was apparently seen as a tempest in a teapot—or a space capsule, as it were—by most of the astronauts, and the controversy it caused faded quickly as the Gemini program moved forward. It was a humorous side effect of the space pilots' ongoing struggle to assert themselves in the mechanized superstructure of the program, and an indication of the vastly different cultures that had produced the astronauts and the engineers responsible for their flights.

The men who flew in America's first space vehicles were for the most part fast-thinking, fast-acting professionals, courageous in the face of imminent personal danger, whose reaction to a crisis situation was in most cases to try something—anything—that seemed as though it might work. Patriotic, understanding of the necessity to take orders, but also sympathetic to the virtues of individual initiative, the astronauts favored the latter approach by a wide margin whenever conflict arose between others' advice and their own intuition. For all their physical exploits as the lead agents of a huge corporate venture, America's first astronauts proved by their actions and words that the program's success or failure ultimately depended at least as much on the proper functioning of the human beings in the spacecraft as it did on the hardware, systems, and computer code.

NASA's vast teams of engineers and administrators and support personnel complemented the astronauts' lessons about the value of the individual with an equally compelling argument for efficient bureaucracy— perhaps providing the only recent example of the term that is not an oxymoron. Bureaucracy worked for NASA in the 1960s; the hierarchical approach to problem solving allowed the agency to respond quickly to problems that arose in the course of the organization's unprecedented venture. When astronauts found themselves confronted with unexpected troubles in space, teams on the ground went to work immediately and efficiently to find solutions by methodical analysis, simulation, and careful weighing of the risks involved. Even where their cultural preferences clashed, the large-scale support of the people on the ground and the closely held intuitions of the astronauts in space meshed exceptionally well, often with miraculous results.

Gemini 4: An American Spacewalk

Such results were the aim of *Gemini 4*, which called for four days in space and the first American EVA. The mission was the first to fly without any of the original astronauts; crew members James McDivitt and Edward White II were both from the second group.

The flight launched on June 3, with White's EVA planned for the fourth orbit. In contrast to the Soviet airlock model, the Gemini approach to spacewalking required that the astronaut exit the craft via one of the hatches that constituted most of each of the capsule's sides. As *Gemini 4* passed over Hawaii, White popped the hatch open and floated out into the vacuum of space, tethered to the capsule and his fellow crew member via a twenty-five-foot tube that passed oxygen to him and in turn allowed him to communicate with McDivitt.

Liberated from every earthly constraint but his protective suit and the thin tether, White reveled in his solo flight. Moving from one direction to the next via a handheld "gun" that propelled him by shooting pressurized oxygen, he thoroughly enjoyed the EVA, and playfully bounced around while McDivitt recorded his actions in a series of remarkable photographs that remain some of the most interesting ever taken in space.

It was only at the end of the twelve-minute EVA that movement became an arduous chore for the spacewalking astronaut. Even though he was free of the problems the narrow Russian airlock had posed for Alexei Leonov during his EVA back in March, White still had to work hard to maneuver himself back into the Gemini capsule. The craft's sleek sides gave him precious little to hang on to as he laboriously pulled himself along, breathing heavily, the exhalation fogging the faceplate of his helmet as he struggled to tumble back through the open hatch. The return to the safe haven of the cockpit took nearly as long as the spacewalk itself, stretching the total EVA to twenty-one minutes. Everyone involved in the effort, on the ground as well as in the capsule, breathed a sigh of relief when McDivitt finally pulled White aboard. The EVA had been a historic first for the United States and an exciting advance, but it was clear that a less stressful method of entering and exiting the capsule would have to be worked out before astronauts could be expected to do useful work while floating in space.[18]

The mission still had a long way to go after White's miraculous stroll. Its primary objectives were to evaluate the effects of prolonged space flight on the craft, the equipment and systems supporting it, and the astronauts. Four days in space gave McDivitt and White a chance to try out NASA's predetermined schedules for working, eating, and sleeping, and to further the maneuvering tests Grissom and Young had begun with *Gemini 3*.

Gemini 4 was a major success. In testing the mettle of its capsule and crew over a long period, it also tempered the systems and equipment of the new mission control center in Houston, which assumed responsibility for flight control for the first time. The good health and high spirits that McDivitt and White displayed after their return to earth assuaged fears about putting astronauts into space for extended periods, and even the partial failure of a planned station-keeping and rendezvous maneuver allowed the ground crew and the astronauts to glean valuable information that would benefit future flights.[19]

One of the few goals not met during the four-day mission was controlled reentry; a fault in the computerized system's memory pushed the reentry test out of reach.

Like the awkward first steps of an infant, the nascent station-keeping attempt and first-ever EVA stretched the potential of the entire organization, raising questions that could, with practice and determination, be answered within a reasonable period of time.

Gemini 5: Pushing the Boundaries

Mercury veteran Gordon Cooper was paired with Charles "Pete" Conrad for *Gemini 5*. The mission's major objective was to double the amount of time in space of *Gemini 4*, again pushing the boundaries of what had previously been achieved, to see what effect the longer stay would have on crew and craft. In the course of its 120 orbits, *Gemini 5* was also scheduled to test the efficacy of fuel cells for the first time (batteries were the primary source of electrical power on previous flights, and would be used for the last time on the short-duration *Gemini 6*) and to perform exercises that would allow ground controllers to evaluate guidance and navigation systems for future rendezvous missions.[20]

Frustrating difficulties seemed to plague the flight from the outset. A launch attempt on August 19 had to be put off when the ground crew was confronted with unexpected problems in loading cryogenic fuel into the fuel cell; liftoff came two days later. Additional problems cropped up with the balky cell once the craft was in orbit, eventually forcing flight controllers to abandon several important rendezvous objectives. To the credit of the crew in the capsule and the controllers on the ground, the mission was able to complete its scheduled 120 orbits, and the astronauts conducted a substantial array of experiments. They splashed down in good health after nearly eight days in space.

NASA administrators added the fuel cell to their growing list of wrinkles that had to be ironed out on the way to Apollo and the moon. Other crucial challenges along the way included rendezvous and docking, and establishing that a flight of as much as two weeks would cause no irreparable damage to the astronauts or to the systems and equipment that would keep them in space.

Gemini 6 and *Gemini 7:* **Rendezvous and Long Duration**

The challenges of rendezvous maneuvers would be addressed head-on in the next flight. *Gemini 6*, with Wally Schirra and Tom Stafford aboard, would be launched shortly after an Atlas rocket put an Agena satellite into orbit; they would then pursue the Agena in space and rendezvous and dock with it.

Frank Borman and James Lovell, both group two astronauts, would then take on the long-duration problem in *Gemini 7*, staying in space for fourteen days.

But NASA's careful planning was thrown into disarray when the Atlas-Agena exploded shortly after it lifted off on October 25. Schirra and Stafford awaited their own launch nearby in *Gemini 6*, but with no target to pursue, their mission was scrubbed.

Several days passed while the space agency pondered what to do next. Then, in an early display of the innovation and boldness that would characterize many of the steps along the way to the moon, NASA officials announced that the *Gemini 6* and *Gemini 7* missions would be combined, undertaken at the same time in December. Since *Gemini 7* would be in space for fourteen days anyway, it would provide a viable target for Schirra and Stafford to track down. Although the vehicles were not yet ready for docking, the rendezvous maneuvers could at least be worked out, and the presence of four astronauts in space at the same time would provide a comfortable cushion of hands-on expertise should any unforeseen circumstances arise.

Gemini 7 launched first, on December 4, 1965. An attempted December 12 launch of *Gemini 6–A*, as the Schirra-Stafford flight had been renamed, failed when the engines of the Titan II launch vehicle shut down. The astronauts' onboard computer indicated that the Titan II had briefly left the launch pad before the malfunction, which meant that the crew would have to forcibly eject themselves from the capsule, but Schirra and Stafford simultaneously agreed that the instruments were in error, and chose to stay inside the spacecraft. It was an excellent example of quick thinking and split-second decision making by the astronauts, and their joint intuition turned out to be accurate. The Titan II remained on the pad, and the capsule and crew remained safely on top of the launch stack.[21]

The mission finally lifted off on December 15. Once they were aloft, Schirra and Stafford made the most of their time in space. They caught up with the target *Gemini 7* during their fourth orbit, and executed the planned rendezvous with great skill and surprising ease. Acting as the pursuing craft, *Gemini 6–A* performed flawless station keeping with the passive *Gemini 7*, Schirra and Stafford managing to stay in close proximity with Borman and Lovell for more than five hours and several trips around the earth. The two craft floated alongside each other at distances ranging from 1 to 295 feet during the exercise, which constituted a major success for the mission and a significant relief for the program, as the Gemini craft overcame one of the major challenges to the eventual moon flights.[22]

Their objectives accomplished in fine form after more than a year of training, mission preparation, and launch delays, Schirra and Stafford brought the *Gemini 6–A* back to earth after a little more than a single day in space.

Borman and Lovell continued on for the remainder of their planned stay, splashing down on December 18. The combined success brought the year to a close on a remarkably high note for NASA, validating the overall direction of the space program and providing valuable experience and information for the future.

Losses on Both Sides

The Soviets experienced a serious setback in January 1966 when Sergei Korolev died. Vasily Mishin replaced him as the chief director of the Russian moon program, which faltered through much of the year as teams of engineers struggled to work through problems with the new Soyuz spacecraft, which included a command module and lunar lander similar to those of the American Apollo project. The Soviets also put enormous engineering resources into development of the N-1 launch vehicle, effectively betting their future in the moon race on the massive booster. Test flights of the N-1 were scheduled to begin in the third quarter of 1967, at the same time the United States would begin testing the Saturn V.[23]

According to the U.S. space agency's plan, 1966 would feature NASA's final preliminaries before the last lap to the moon could begin in earnest. The last round of Geminis—five more flights—were scheduled to fly by year's end, bringing back answers to the last remaining questions about the safety and feasibility of setting human beings down on the lunar surface.

The first casualties of that grand journey were astronauts Elliot See and Charles Bassett. See, a group two selection in 1962, and Bassett, of group three, had been selected as the crew of *Gemini 9*. They had endured the long preparation and rigorous training necessary to get assigned to a mission, and were to fly in space for the first time in May. But it was not to be. The two astronauts were killed in an airplane crash on February 28 while flying to the McDonnell Aircraft plant in St. Louis. The sad ironies of the deaths were overwhelming. They had worked hard and gotten within easy distance of their long-sought opportunity, only to be dealt their grim fate in an altogether earthly flying vehicle. And yet, by their service and in their passing, they gave the space program positive examples of the dedication that distinguished the work of all the astronauts. The accident gave everyone connected with NASA a distinct moment of pause, to reflect on the hugeness of their collective aims and the fragile humanity of the people who were the vanguard of their most cherished dreams.[24]

Tom Stafford and Gene Cernan—the backup crew for *Gemini 9*— were flying alongside See and Bassett in a second T-38 when the crash occurred. They watched in horror as the first plane fell through the dense fog and crashed just before it was to have landed at the McDonnell facility.[25] Yet the grim reality of the situation dictated that Stafford and Cernan move up to become the prime crew for *Gemini 9*.

Gemini 8: Near-Disaster

Amid the shock of the accident that claimed See and Bassett, the first mission of the new year—*Gemini 8*—was launched on March 16. Crew members Neil Armstrong and David Scott were charged with working out the details of rendezvous and docking, basically fulfilling the profile of the original *Gemini 6* mission, which had been aborted when the target vehicle exploded after launch.[26]

This time around, the launch of the Agena target went smoothly, and Armstrong and Scott followed a short time later. All went well up to the moment when they caught up with the Agena and locked onto it, slaying another dragon that had previously stood at the door to NASA's lunar aims.

Cheers and congratulations went around at mission control when *Gemini 8* locked and docked. The hard part was done; some docked-vehicle maneuvering would follow, with the tiny spacecraft effortlessly pushing along the Agena, which was more than twice its weight, in the vacuum of space. Then the astronauts began their swing over China, which would put them out of reach of ground tracking stations and momentarily cut their communications with mission control. Although it was only a brief interruption, the blackout marked the beginning of a frightening ordeal for Armstrong and Scott, with nearly tragic results.

Inexplicably, the combined Gemini-Agena balked, suddenly and violently spinning, shaking, and rolling in a dizzy, uncontrolled spiral. Armstrong and Scott quickly ran through the prescribed procedures that should have brought the craft back under their control, but the spinning continued at an even faster rate. Faced with the possibility of imminent disaster, they decided to let go of the Agena, figuring that the undocking would also detach them from whatever was causing the problem.

Amazingly, when they jettisoned their target, their rate of rotation increased. They were now spinning a full turn every second, and the spacecraft wasn't responding. Controllers on the ground were shocked to hear Armstrong, coming out of the communications blackout, describe the sudden turn of events: "We have a serious problem here . . . We're tumbling end over end up here. We've disengaged from the Agena."

With precious little time left before the dizzying, out-of-control gyrations of their spacecraft would cause the two astronauts to lose consciousness, they decided to try some drastic measures. They first cut the capsule's power, and when that didn't work, Armstrong fired the retrorockets, whose use would normally be reserved for reentry, and shut down the thrusters that would have been used for the planned maneuvers with the docked Agena. By countering the push of the thrusters with the force of the retro-rockets, he was able to gain enough stability to slow the spin to a survivable rate.

Once they were able to better evaluate the situation, the astronauts and the ground controllers realized that the spinning had been set in motion when one of the maneuvering thrusters had inexplicably remained open while the rest had shut down. When the thruster finally exhausted its fuel, the spinning stopped and the crew was again able to take control. But it had been a near-miss. If the retro-rockets had not stabilized the craft enough for Armstrong and Scott to remain conscious and outlast the stuck thruster, they would not have survived. Quick thinking and immediate action had once again proved the value of the astronauts' experience and training.

NASA's safety rules mandated that the early use of the reentry system would cut the rest of the mission short to preserve as much of the remaining fuel as possible for reentry. Preparations for a quick return to earth began as soon as mission control was sure that the craft was again under the astronauts' control.

Armstrong and Scott once more found themselves out of contact during their return as they hurled toward an emergency recovery site in the Pacific that was out of reach of tracking stations. The reentry and recovery went well, though, and they were safely retrieved by the USS *Mason* about three hours after they hit the water. They had been in space for a little less than ten hours.

Although the mission had not accomplished NASA's goal of validating its rendezvous and docking techniques, it did provide the astronauts and mission control with remarkable insight into the resilience of the program's systems and equipment, and the intuitive ability of the crew to deal with emergencies.[27]

The mission postmortem issued by NASA flight director Chris Kraft cited an electrical short in the capsule's control system as the cause of the thruster staying open when it should have shut. Kraft also singled out Armstrong's remarkable performance and lauded the crew for their bravery in overcoming the nearly fatal mishap.[28]

Gemini 9: The "Alligator" and the Astronaut Maneuvering Unit

Reliable techniques for rendezvous, docking, and spacewalking had still not been successfully "road-tested" in space. Tom Stafford and Gene Cernan set out to shorten the list of ongoing problems in each of those areas when they lifted off in *Gemini 9* on June 3. The Agena target vehicle that they were scheduled to rendezvous with had failed to reach orbit in mid-May, so their mission was delayed for two weeks, eventually following the successful launch of a standby target on June 1.

They had no difficulty catching up to the target, but when they did, it presented them with an unwelcome surprise. A long, narrow shroud designed to protect the vehicle's docking mechanism had only partially opened, rendering the Agena useless for docking purposes. Its odd appearance, like that of some weird metallic reptile with half-breached jaws, led Stafford to jokingly dub it the "angry alligator."[29]

In spite of their uncooperative target, the astronauts made the best of things, and successfully performed station-keeping exercises and three different types of rendezvous during their forty-five orbits.

More arduous was Cernan's abbreviated two-hour EVA. Suffering much of the same disorienting bouncing and rolling as Ed White had during his spacewalk a year earlier, Cernan struggled to control his movement outside the craft. Laboriously pulling himself along on the life-sustaining tether and alternately holding on to the capsule with one hand, he eventually reached the experimental astronaut maneuvering unit (AMU) that he was supposed to try out for the first time in space.

Fatigue, stiffness and a blinding fog on the inside of his faceplate wore Cernan down during the cumbersome exercise. Weighing in on the cautious side of its concerns about his safety, mission control quickly agreed to cut the EVA short when Cernan wondered aloud if the AMU trial might be abandoned. Including the time it took him to climb back into the capsule, Cernan had performed his extravehicular duties for an exhausting two hours and seven minutes.[30]

Other than the disappointment of not being able to try out the planned docking maneuvers and the AMU, the flight was a success. Stafford and Cernan had salvaged a difficult situation, and their maneuvering included a simulated lunar module rendezvous. Progress, even of a limited, halting sort, was clearly being made.

Gemini 10: On Target

John Young made his second trip in a Gemini capsule with the *Gemini 10* mission, joined by group three astronaut Michael Collins. They lifted off on July 18, and this time, the target vehicle performed flawlessly, finally providing a real opportunity for a full tryout of the rendezvous and docking procedures. Both exercises went well, and a subsequent test of the Agena's engine propelled the *Gemini 10* capsule into a higher orbit. It was the first time the propulsion system of the target vehicle had been used to set a manned craft in motion.

From their new perspective, Collins performed a "stand-up" EVA, so named because it allowed the astronaut to brace himself in the frame of an open hatch, rather than venturing fully outside the craft. He spent a total of forty-nine minutes in the capsule doorway, capturing images of the heavens on film. The picture-taking duty was a prelude to his main EVA, a fully external foray to retrieve a micrometeorite experiment from the *Gemini 8* Agena target vehicle.

This second walk was more difficult, but Collins was able to accomplish his task and return to the safety of the *Gemini 10* capsule within thirty-nine minutes. The mission, a major advance for the program and a welcome success after the exceptionally tense moments of *Gemini 8* and *Gemini 9*, ended on July 21 with a near-perfect splashdown in the Atlantic.[31]

Gemini 11: Apollo in Miniature

The first Gemini to successfully mimic most of the major maneuvers necessary to Apollo was *Gemini 11*. Commanded by Pete Conrad, in his second tour in space, with pilot Richard Gordon, the flight began on September 12 and quickly achieved its first precedent-breaking objective. During its first orbit, the Gemini rendezvoused with its Agena target and docked in the same fashion as the later Apollo command craft would dock with their lunar modules during their first orbit. Pulling the two craft together with surprising ease, both Conrad and Gordon tried out the docking maneuver.

Following the successful rendezvous and docking, Gordon exited the Gemini to perform an innovative experiment: during his EVA, he would attach a one-hundred-foot tether between the space capsule and the Agena target vehicle. Tying two vehicles together was an intriguing idea, as it might allow long periods of close travel without the need for the occupants to actively perform station-keeping duties.[32]

The EVA was, once again, a long walk. A bit of humor intervened at one point when Gordon straddled the long, thin target vehicle as he struggled to attach the tether. Conrad shouted, "Ride 'em, cowboy," as Gordon bounced along the smooth edge of the Agena. Once the tether was affixed, though, the commander became all business as he helped pull his exhausted crewmate back into the Gemini. The EVA was cut short at thirty-three minutes.

The tethered flight went well, and Gordon conducted a second EVA, this one of the more pleasant stand-up variety, that lasted about two hours. It was apparently so pleasant, in fact, that the astronauts reportedly slept through a portion of it, Conrad inside the capsule and Gordon floating in the hatchway.

At the end of the three-day mission, *Gemini 11* achieved one final triumph when it accomplished a fully automatic reentry, utilizing one more of the methods that would be needed to ensure the success of Apollo.[33]

Gemini 12: Solving the EVA Dilemma

Among its other objectives, the last Gemini flight had as its main goal the vanquishing of the difficult EVA—the last remaining bogey among the procedures that were essential to the program's future. Should astronauts eventually reach the moon, their ability to work outside their spacecraft would be essential to the mission in both symbolic and practical terms. And closer to home, there was a safety benefit to the option of a hands-on fix in an emergency, or even the eventual possibility of a rescue mission being achieved via an emergency EVA from one craft to another.

Fortunately, the *Gemini 12* crew was well chosen for the task. James Lovell flew his second Gemini mission, accompanied by Edwin "Buzz" Aldrin, who had been selected as part of the third group of astronauts in 1963. During training for his scheduled EVA, Aldrin threw himself into the problems described by White, Cernan, Collins, and Gordon. He carefully studied the mechanics of moving about in space, and devised innovative simulations to try out his ideas about how to improve the process. His success or failure would be NASA's last shot at smoothing out its EVA procedures before the first Apollo flight.[34]

With the benefit of Aldrin's experiments and the considerable input of the previous spacewalkers, the program's engineers set out to improve the odds of a successful EVA by adding a large variety of handholds, footholds, and railings to the Gemini capsule and the target Agena. They also devised a waist tether that doubled as a sort of cosmic toolbelt, and added shoe restraints to the Gemini in the area where Aldrin would be working.[35]

Gemini 12 launched on November 11, 1966. Its rendezvous, docking, and station-keeping exercises went smoothly, although some docked maneuvers had to be canceled due to an anomaly with the Agena target.

Aldrin's first EVA was easy, as he stood in the hatch, enjoying the view and the relative stability of being half in and half out of the spacecraft. It was his second venture that put all the preparation to the test. The first difference became evident after just a short while, as Aldrin moved slowly, deliberately, and with frequent stops along the way as he moved outside the Gemini craft, dragging a tether toward the target Agena.

He made expert use of the equipment and techniques he'd practiced during his long preparation back home; perhaps most tellingly, he seemed mentally adjusted to the task at hand. Methodically selecting tools from their spot on the waist tether, focusing his energy on each new job, whether it was turning a bolt with a wrench or attaching the tether to the Agena, Aldrin worked carefully and without hurrying. By the time he wrapped up his final moments outside *Gemini 12*, he had achieved a new record EVA duration of five hours and thirty minutes, and he had proven that working in space was both possible and practical.[36]

By upping his total time in space to 425 hours (the combination of the four-day *Gemini 12* flight and the earlier 14-day *Gemini 7* mission), the affable Lovell also set a new standard, becoming the world's most experienced space traveler up to that point. His continued good health alleviated the fears of NASA's medical teams about the possible ill effects of continued exposure to space and the stress of training for and flying the complex, dangerous missions.

A Closer Moon

Gemini had accomplished a great deal. Its contributions to Apollo were obvious, but it also succeeded in its own right, in a subtler, quieter fashion than Mercury had or Apollo would. Perhaps the main contribution of Project Gemini was that it made spaceflight both real and fantastic at the same time. By launching ten manned flights in a period of twenty months, the project provided the media and the public with a constant source of information about the people, procedures, and aims of the space program, frequently mixing the detached logic of scientific experimentation with alarmingly unexpected human drama.

By the end of 1966, Gemini had made the planned journey to the moon an increasingly likely reality, and a goal that seemed an appropriately hopeful symbol of American aspirations on earth. Widespread ques-

tioning of the nation's involvement in the Vietnam War had not yet begun, and the gains of the civil rights movement, coupled with Lyndon
Johnson's "Great Society" social programs, sparked a vigorous national
debate about how to create a fairer, more equitable social order.

Given the mood of the times, the space program epitomized the nation's
most generous instincts. The fact that the United States had caught up to
and surpassed the Soviets in the space race was a source of national
pride for a majority of Americans, but there were indications that it was
also becoming less important than the promise that human beings would
soon walk on the moon. Thanks in no small part to Project Gemini, the
American public began to display an overarching concern with the cosmic importance of traveling in the heavens.

As it wound its way forward, trying out the various procedures and
systems and equipment deemed necessary for its big brother, Apollo,
Gemini gave the American space odyssey a new image, broader in demeanor than that allowed by the earlier space race obsessions, and no-
bler in character. It embraced and celebrated the increasingly realistic
possibility that the day of landing on the moon would come to pass
sooner rather than later, and the attendant reality that this new adventure
just might in some way alter humanity's perception of its past, and its
dream of the future.

4

Apollo 1: Lives in Eclipse

Officially given life by formal NASA decree in July 1960, the Apollo program would in the final three years of the decade concentrate humanity's fundamental longing to explore the heavens—probably felt even in the nascent consciousness of one of *Homo sapiens'* long-ago hairy ancestors as he or she gazed upward in first awareness of the moonlit sky—into the success or failure of a massive machine, hurled into space at an unthinkable speed, with three comparatively frail and tiny individuals inside. For all the grand romance and futuristic visions, it was the safe passage of those three individuals that was the foremost mission of all those associated with the journey in even the smallest, most prosaic capacity.

The Apollo project represented America's most idealistic aspirations during an increasingly confusing time. It combined the nation's old romantic ideals of exploration and adventure with the pervasive promise of forward-looking technology, while also reaffirming the importance of the individual in even the most complex corporate undertaking. Paradoxically, and even as the image of one of its own actually setting foot on the moon began to emerge more clearly, the general public was at the same time beginning to face some unsettling misgivings about the course its government was pursuing by precipitously escalating the nation's involvement in the Vietnam War.

The two defining elements of 1960s America, the moon landing and the war, were intricately interwoven in the politics of the day. For a while, it was politically fashionable to be for one (the initially patriotic war against Communism) and against the other (the expensive, often-delayed space program); as the decade progressed, the roles reversed, as previously prowar politicians came to see the effort as at best a losing proposition and at worst a senseless bloodbath, and the voices decrying the space program's cost and scheduling faded into silence as Apollo edged ever closer to the surface of the moon.

For all its technology and grand ambition, all its parts and poetry, Apollo's mission really was as simple as John Kennedy had originally envisioned it: to land a man on the moon and return him safely to earth, and to accomplish the feat before the end of the decade. Whatever the technology's achievements, and whatever heroic trappings a tragic mishap might possess, Apollo would represent humanity's most dismal conceit if it resulted in the loss of astronauts in space or on the moon. The specter of a human satellite circling the earth for ages to come, or the desolate moonscape as a final resting place, was simply too horrible an end for a drama so noble and so long in unfolding.

By the dawn of 1967, there was no middle path for NASA or its astronauts; there only could be the righteous confirmation of a safe journey or the awful condemnation of lives sacrificed in vain. All paths led to the moon, and the trip had to be completed before New Year's Day three years hence, so that Kennedy's mandate would be fulfilled.

The Saturn V Rocket

The program began, as would each flight to the moon, with an enormous rocket, the Saturn V. Consisting of three separate stages intricately engineered and developed by different manufacturers, the Saturn V came together under the guidance of Wernher von Braun at the Marshall Space Flight Center in Alabama. The first stage, dubbed the S-IC, was the responsibility of the Boeing Corporation. Its five engines powered by a mix of some 330,000 gallons of liquid oxygen and 200,000 gallons of kerosene, the 150–foot-tall S-IC provided enormous lift for the two rocket stages that sat atop it, as well as the service and command modules above them.

For the second stage, the S-II, the contractor was North American Aviation, which was also building the command module that would house the astronauts in space. North American developed a new engine for the S-II in order to take advantage of highly efficient liquid hydrogen fuel; five such engines powered the finished S-II.

The uppermost piece of the launch rocket was the S-IVB, designed by the Douglas Aircraft Company. Its single engine was also fueled by liquid hydrogen, but was designed for in-flight thrust, to put the spacecraft into earth orbit or to set it on its way to the moon. It was also the seat of the Saturn V's guidance and control nerve center, an immensely complex IBM-built computer responsible for tracking and controlling virtually every aspect of the huge rocket's performance during launch and separation of the stages.[1]

The *Apollo 1* Crew

The men assigned the task of opening the Apollo era were veterans Gus Grissom and Ed White, and group three astronaut Roger Chaffee, who was to fly in space for the first time. Standard-bearers for the program destined to culminate in realizing the ancient dream of humanity's first contact with another world, the initial Apollo astronauts were subject to intense pressure both within the space agency and externally, from the media and the general public. The Mercury and Gemini projects had at the very least evened up the space race with the Soviets; in fact, the success of those programs had made the possibility of being first on the moon seem a near-certainty, provided Apollo could match the speed and efficiency of its predecessors. NASA was certainly optimistic as the year began, with the launch of *Apollo 1*—the first step in the last push toward the moon—scheduled for February 21, 1967.[2]

The objectives of the initial launch were relatively simple, although somewhat daunting for an entirely new spacecraft of such enormous complexity. As the first in the Apollo series, the mission's primary task was to prove the spacecraft worthy of flight by completing fourteen days in earth orbit, and to then test its ability to endure the same rigors of reentry that the later Apollos would on their way back from the moon.

But there were problems. In sharp contrast to the pleasant "company line" that the space agency promoted to its supporters and detractors alike, development of the Apollo command module was not proceeding quickly enough, and the scheduled launch seemed in peril. Even so,

NASA's "good news" policy was born less of duplicity than of necessity, in the face of all the old questions about the space program being raised anew during the interim between the end of Gemini and the start of Apollo. The questions were the same as before: couldn't the money be better spent on earthly ventures? Was it really necessary for the astronauts to reach the moon by the end of the decade? Couldn't far cheaper unmanned probes accomplish just as much without endangering human lives?[3]

As always, the astronauts themselves were the agency's best defense against criticism. However deeply held one's reservations were about the logic and goals of the space program, the smiling faces of the hardworking, dedicated astronauts were irresistible to all but those most adamantly opposed to the program or the agency, or those who'd simply grown too cynical to take more than a passing interest in romantic adventure or epic drama of any sort. Soldiers of peace bent on exploring the darkness of space in the idealistic hope that such adventure might somehow further the cause of our humble little blue world, the astronauts brought a new kind of nobility to the image of the bluff hero the nation had come to know from its films and television programs. Filled out in flesh and blood, suffering a lonely yearning for something truly new that could be adequately understood only by his fellow sufferers, the astronaut was the personification of the heroic American archetype.

Grissom, White, and Chaffee

The particular crew of *Apollo 1* definitively represented their fellows, as though cast to type. Chaffee, for instance, was the epitome of the earnest young All-American about to validate his superiors' belief in his obvious potential. By taking his place alongside the first select few who would meet the risks necessary for the opportunity to fly in space, he would contribute to the knowledge and experience that would eventually land an American on the moon, and who knew what after that? As he posed in his bulky space suit for the photographs NASA needed to help convince the world that *Apollo 1* would proceed as planned, he could hardly have imagined just how awful a price those risks would demand, or how integral a contribution he and his crewmen would make to the program's ultimate outcome.[4]

Ed White was probably more relaxed in the glaring spotlight of public attention. He'd had ample experience with public hero worship when he became the first American to walk in space, during the June 1965 flight of *Gemini 4*. He projects a smooth, relaxed confidence in NASA's Apollo photos, a warm, broad smile adorning the face previously hidden by his reflective visor in the famous series of photos from his spacewalk. If the images can be trusted as an accurate depiction of his emotions at the time, White surely must have been looking forward to his role in Apollo. While his place in history had already been secured thanks to his Gemini exploits, his smile suggests the forward-looking confidence embodied by so many of the astronauts as they addressed new assignments. In any case, his is a comforting countenance, full of joy and anticipation.[5]

Gus Grissom, of course, had demonstrated the astronauts' courage when, after nearly drowning in his doomed Mercury capsule, he returned to space with John Young on the first manned Gemini mission. Now he would have the honor of being commander of the first Apollo. Present at the creation as one of the original Mercury Seven, Grissom was familiar to millions of Americans, who were no doubt reassured by his broad grin beaming out at them from the official NASA photos as they picked up their daily newspapers to read of the crew's preparations.[6]

Tragically, the earlier mishap would reassert itself, in a most horrible and grotesque fashion, at the dawn of the Apollo era. In deference to the unexplained malfunction of the explosive hatch door that prematurely popped the covering off Grissom's Mercury capsule and nearly resulted in his drowning, the hatch of the first Apollo was designed with anything but a speedy exit in mind. Where the earlier, explosive version would have blown the door off instantaneously, the only exit from *Apollo 1* required an escaping crew member to pull heavily on three separate release levers in order to get out of the spacecraft in an emergency. The procedure required at least a minute and a half.[7]

Perhaps given more time, the astronauts or NASA or the capsule's manufacturer might have addressed the risks posed by such a system early on, as well as the myriad other risks involved in hundreds of other potentially serious malfunctions and equipment failures. But all these always had to be weighed against the time constraints inherent in the manic rush to reach the moon.

The intense strain of the moment cannot be appreciated properly in retrospect, as the time-to-market pressures routinely faced by equipment manufacturers and government agencies were telescoped a thousandfold by the nature and purpose of the product being built. The command module, after all, was the cradle that would harbor successive teams of astronauts as they ventured into the unknown with the explosive force of a 160–million-horsepower blast, and later returned to earth at a speed of 25,000 miles per hour. As the designated manufacturer of the Apollo command module, North American Aviation faced the double challenge of producing a defect-free vehicle and doing it as quickly as possible. Somewhere along the way, the secondary consideration of adhering to the schedule overtook the first.[8]

Risking Failure . . . or Worse

The command module that astronauts Grissom, White, and Chaffee entered on January 27, 1967 was nowhere near defect-free. In fact, as Alan Shepard and Deke Slayton pointed out in their joint memoir *Moon Shot*, Grissom, as commander, not only was aware of the plague of problems inherent in his spacecraft, but also voiced his dissatisfaction frequently and openly. In fact, it is obvious that all three astronauts were keenly aware of the enormous risk involved even in testing out so complex a vehicle under the circumstances.[9]

And NASA knew as well. As Shepard and Slayton report, Apollo spacecraft manager Joseph Shea had candidly admitted during a press conference that the program as a whole had seen thousands of failures of one sort or another, and he expressed concern that some might have an impact on the astronauts' safety. Of course, he had no way of knowing just how prescient such concerns would be.[10]

The procedures that day were intended to confirm that the command module, service module, and launch systems could each operate on their own power. The test called for the command module to be prepared just as it would be prior to launch, with the astronauts in the cabin, their space suits enveloped within an atmosphere of pure oxygen, necessary for the elimination of airborne contaminants. The communications, electrical, and cooling systems would also be tested during the run-through, as they would be required in the process of powering up the vehicle. Though originally planned as an unmanned test, with the astronauts taking part only after everything had been deemed adequately safe and appropriately functional, the vagaries of the schedule dictated that the unmanned test be scrapped in favor of a full workout with the astronauts in place, just as they would be during the fast-approaching launch.

At least the run-through would pinpoint specific areas that required further modifications. NASA's requests for modifications had become increasingly frequent and maddeningly numerous as more and more difficulties were discovered, and the effect of all the changes was felt throughout the operation. Just a day earlier, there had been fifty-six major changes in procedure that the astronauts would now have to deal with, even as they wrestled with a multitude of other balky bits of equipment whose failure during the actual launch could result in consequences ranging from the mildly annoying to the potentially life-threatening.

The Test

Despite all their misgivings, Grissom, White, and Chaffee, true to their training and their faith in the systems, procedures, and personnel that had thus far served the space program so well, gamely entered the command module, seated atop its two-stage Saturn IB rocket (the IB would be sufficient to launch the astronauts into earth orbit so they could test the Apollo machinery; the three-stage Saturn V would be necessary for the later moonbound launches). As the three crew members adjusted their posture to fit the couches from which they would operate the capsule's controls, they were also settling in atop a thick tangle of bundled wires, many of which provided electricity for the craft's various systems, and at least some of which were frayed, compressed, flattened, or nicked. The complex, double-hulled hatch was sealed, pure oxygen was pumped in to purify the cabin's atmosphere, and the test began.

More problems appeared. Literally aware of something strange in the air, the astronauts were disturbed by a sour odor that filled the spacecraft's cabin. The crew duly reported the problem, albeit with some hint of annoyance that there were once again unexpected difficulties with systems that should by then have been error-free. The spacecraft's environmental control system managed to remove the odor, only to have it flood back in again, then be swept out once more, no doubt wearing the crew's patience a little thinner in the process.[11]

Once the mysterious odor had been removed, the mock countdown procedure began again. The crew, the workers on the platform surrounding the spacecraft, and two separate teams of NASA administrative personnel who were monitoring the test remotely all pooled their collective knowledge and effort to speed the trial along. But like some grotesque, obstinate beast suddenly beset by an awareness of its own shortcomings, the capsule continued to produce obstructions that threw the countdown into disarray.

Next it was the craft's communications system that faltered, with the words passed to and from the capsule's commander and the nearby administrative teams ravaged and eventually lost in a harsh, grating static. Five hours had passed since the crew had first entered the spacecraft, five long, frustrating hours in which the test's main objectives receded a little farther with each new obstacle. As Shepard and Slayton describe the day's progress, there was some consideration of quitting altogether when the problem with Grissom's microphone arose, but as the test's main goals could still be achieved in spite of the fault in the communications system, the supervisory team decided to work around the difficulty as much as possible and continue the power-up procedure.[12]

Like the millions of small, seemingly inconsequential decisions that had preceded it on the long path to the moon, the choice to continue the test was made with the best of intentions. It likely took into consideration the pressures of the tight schedule, and perhaps the need for the crew and support staff to achieve some concrete progress toward their goal after suffering so much frustration. Apart from all that had gone before, it would have meant little to what would happen next; but as the last of a long line of relatively minor mistakes, it would be the catalyst for horrific tragedy.

As the astronauts lay on their couches in the *Apollo 1* cabin, awash in an atmosphere of highly flammable pure oxygen on top of a forest of twisted wire bundles, some small fault in the electrical system produced a spark, leaping up from the floor on Gus Grissom's side of the capsule. As far as anyone investigating the incident could later determine, a small fire resulted, burning for perhaps ten seconds before igniting a massive holocaust. Fed by the oxygen, flames quickly engulfed the entire innards of the small cabin.

There were precious few moments for last words. Gus Grissom shouted, "I've got a fire in the cockpit," preceded and followed by a single word first from Ed White and then from Roger Chaffee: "Fire!" Long years of training took over; the three astronauts fell immediately to their emergency tasks, Grissom frantically trying to release the lever that would vent the cabin of the oxygen atmosphere, White heaving hard against the workings of the inner hatch, Chaffee valiantly trying to maintain communications even as the fire raged violently all around him. In a single, horrible instant, the cabin was awash in a killing heat, later estimated at anywhere from 1,400 to 2,500 degrees Fahrenheit.

The fire overcame the three astronauts in less than ten seconds.

Witness to Apocalypse

Terrified by what was happening to the three men whose care was their most sacred concern, management and support personnel from NASA and North American Aviation caught a brief flash of what was happening inside the capsule as it played out on their closed-circuit television monitors. The images they now saw on the screens that had been their window into the astronauts' world were nightmarish and alien. Although they wouldn't know it for sure for several more minutes, the apocalypse had come and gone even more quickly than they could register their own shock. And it took with it the lives of Gus Grissom, Ed White, and Roger Chaffee.

Those closest to the capsule, the teams working on the structure around it, courageously lived up to their dedication to the astronauts, scrambling toward the seething spacecraft with no thought of their own safety. They fought the fire as well as they could, not knowing that it had already done its worst. And they filled the hospital afterward, suffering in various degrees from burns, smoke inhalation, and shock.

The dismay and sadness felt by all those who had known and worked with the three astronauts were shared by the nation at large, as the cheery images of NASA's publicity photos were replaced in people's minds by descriptions of the fire, the thwarted rescue efforts, and the astronauts' funerals. A few days after the fire, Lieutenant Colonel Grissom and Lieutenant Commander Chaffee were buried in Arlington National Cemetery; Lieutenant Colonel White was buried at his alma mater, the U.S. Military Academy at West Point, New York.

A Parallel Soviet Tragedy

As if the sadness of the moment were somehow insufficient evidence that the adventure of space exploration was at its root an epic of individual human exploits rather than a mere marker of technological achievement, the Soviet space program was also marred by a tragic loss of life just three short months after the *Apollo 1* fire.

In its own efforts to test out its systems and equipment and provide its cosmonauts with the experience necessary to land on the moon, the Soviet program was proceeding at a rapid rate with flights similar to those the Americans had planned. Central to the program was a mission calling for the docking of two separate craft in space and the transfer of crew members between the two capsules.

Soyuz 1, the spacecraft intended to be the first of the two to link up, was launched on April 23, 1967, piloted by Vladimir Komarov. The experienced Komarov had flown in space previously as the commander of the forward-looking *Voskhod 1*, the first craft to carry a three-man crew, in October 1964.

Soyuz 2, with a two-man crew, was to follow Komarov into space the day after his ascent, but the flight was canceled when his craft experienced problems soon after launch. *Soyuz 1* first suffered from a loss of electrical power when one of its solar panels failed to unfold fully, and then apparently also developed problems with its computer system, resulting in an inability to stabilize its flight. After fifteen orbits, Komarov was ordered to abort the mission and return to earth. He made several attempts to do so, apparently taking over the craft's controls manually, and valiantly fought against his recalcitrant capsule throughout his last three passes around the earth.

Although he expertly handled the spacecraft's reentry under nearly impossible circumstances, Komarov had no way of untangling the parachute of his descent module, which deployed improperly and failed to slow the capsule's descent. The gifted, courageous cosmonaut was killed instantly when the craft, spinning wildly out of control, crashed horribly to earth and was engulfed in flames produced by its exploding retrorockets. In normal flight, the rockets would have gently slowed the craft just prior to landing.

The crash would ground the Soviets' manned progress toward the moon for the next year and a half. Perhaps more important, and yet ultimately unheeded, were the implications of the accident for both the USSR and the United States in its terrible symmetry to the American Apollo tragedy. Komarov's loss was yet another reminder that the great promise of space flight was a legacy that would be shared in both its success and its sorrow by all humanity. An urgently poetic parallel to the loss of the *Apollo 1* crew, the *Soyuz 1* crash underscored the grand nature of the adventure being undertaken, as well as the gravity of its risks.[13]

Even as the rhetoric of the space race was leading the efforts of both countries ever closer to the moon, the astronauts and cosmonauts shared an understanding, even from so great a distance, of the unforgiving trials of the long journey. But the concerns of the earthbound remained; when the United States offered to send two of its astronauts to Komarov's funeral in a rare display of official compassion toward its superpower enemy, its gesture was politely refused by the Soviets. Even the sadness of their shared loss could only momentarily deter the competition be-tween the two great space powers; the cold war, the space race, and the Vietnam conflict continued apace.

Less than a month after Komarov's death, the Soviets selected the cosmonauts they intended to land on the moon. But it was the failure of the massive N-1 rocket, the Soviet parallel to the Americans' Saturn V, that definitively cost the USSR its chance to be the first nation to land a human being on the lunar surface. Two N-1 tests were conducted in 1969, both resulting in spectacular explosions. Fortunately, neither in-volved manned spacecraft.[14]

Impact of the *Apollo 1* Fire

Following as it did the long buildup of the successful Mercury and Gemini programs and the intense pressures of public attention and media scru-tiny that immediately preceded it, the *Apollo 1* fire threw NASA and its plans for a lunar landing into immediate eclipse. The space agency's achievements were occulted by doubts large and small about its ability to protect the astronauts from harm.

The immediate effect of the tragedy was the complete halt of every-thing and everyone associated with the Apollo program. All plans to fly into space, to reach the moon for the grand adventure of the effort or the baser motive of achieving some advantage—real or perceived—over the Soviets, were now brought to a sudden stop.

The fire changed the very manner in which the future of space explo-ration could be publicly discussed. Debate about the efficacy of the space program, doubts about the value of its achievements or the logic of its goals, could never again be the theoretical disagreements of political grandstanders, television news commentators, or newspaper editorial-ists. Partisan argument would henceforth have to be addressed with a new seriousness, not as a rhetorical exercise, but with an all-too-acute awareness that the conclusions to be reached were indeed issues of life and death.[15]

Even to speak of the tragedy as an "accident" was not entirely appro-priate; certainly no one had anticipated the fire, so in that sense it had obviously been accidental, but it was at the same time a markedly differ-ent experience from that of the unfortunate who is killed in a typical car crash or some similar event. The astronauts were acutely aware of the risks they faced each day, in training, in preparing for a flight, or during an actual mission. Despite the obvious and constant hazards involved, they courageously faced each new task with quiet confidence in the thousands of support personnel, systems, and components whose expert functioning they relied upon. To speak of the fire solely in terms of its accidental occurrence was to miss to some degree the poignancy of the astronauts' sacrifice and the nature of their courage.

As is often the case with bureaucracy, when confusion reigns, institutions fall back on routine and procedure, committees and commitments. Although no one was quite sure what impact the fire would have on the program's future, NASA gave some hint of its preferred direction when it announced on February 4, the same day that the astronauts' cause of death was revealed as "asphyxiation due to smoke inhalation," that it planned to go ahead with three unmanned Apollo flights during the remainder of 1967.

Those who would later decry the haste and risk of the Apollo program could convincingly argue that all the relatively minor difficulties that had plagued the effort to this point had been inevitably leading toward disaster and needlessly endangering the astronauts' lives. Similar arguments would be made again nearly twenty years hence, in the wake of the *Challenger* disaster. But the differences between the two tragedies were as vast as the differences in the purpose of the program, and indeed the agency itself, in the 1960s and the 1980s.

Such debate was misinformed or even disingenuous in regard to Apollo, in that it did not fully account for the nature of the program at the time. Despite the harsh trappings of the space race, there was enough goodwill inherent in the general aim to explore space, and to reach the moon, to shield Apollo from questions about its underlying moral rectitude or rightness of purpose. For all the debate regarding the advantages of unmanned Surveyors versus manned Apollos, and the sometimes studied misgivings of politicians about the cost of the manned space program, it was generally understood that Apollo's great achievement would be human exploration of the moon. A goal perhaps outrageously romantic for a society as technologically advanced as the United States in the 1960s, it was nonetheless an achievement that the nation as a whole was willing to support with the two commodities most important to its successful attainment: money and attention.

As a result, it was the only goal NASA could pursue at the time. The fire would have to be transformed into a beacon for the future, or else the moon would have to be left untouched—at least untouched by Americans—for the foreseeable future.

The Investigation

The first difficulty in dealing with the tragedy was the lack of an appropriate means for describing and assessing such an unprecedented event. Descriptions of the facts were relatively easy; indeed, the facts were relatively few. Films and recordings of the fire were sealed immediately after the flames ebbed; photographs were made at the time, and of virtually every component of the spacecraft as each piece was removed afterward; and an official board of inquiry was appointed to sift through the massive amount of data, in the hope that some definitive explanation of the fire's cause would eventually be found.

It was not to be. Despite an exhaustive inquiry and the 3,000–page report the board released in early April, the exact cause of the fire that engulfed *Apollo 1* was never found. The general conclusion was that an electrical fault had ignited some of the capsule's faulty wiring, with the resulting flames spreading quickly onto the large amounts of combustible material that had been used throughout the dangerously sealed cabin; the extremely flammable oxygen atmosphere was ignited instantaneously. Highly critical of NASA and North American Aviation, the report found numerous faults with the spacecraft's design, engineering, and manufacture. One particularly infamous example of shoddy workmanship that the board offered as evidence of lax quality control was the discovery of "foreign object debris" (FOD in the acronym-obsessed aerospace jargon) within the spacecraft: a wrench socket was found on the floor of the cabin amid the bundles of twisted, melted wire.[16]

But what mattered more than finding the exact cause of the fire was gaining as ironclad a reassurance as possible that it would not happen again. The long-term result of the fire and the investigation into its cause was an overhaul of the specific systems involved and a thorough examination of all those that would play a role in the program's future. The changes were detailed in the more than 1,300 modifications that NASA demanded in the spacecraft and its attendant procedures. The oxygen environment was diluted with nitrogen for a safer cabin atmosphere on the ground, with the move to pure oxygen delayed until the craft was in space, where the chance of fire would be significantly lower. Space suits were made fireproof. Combustible materials were removed and replaced with nonflammable alternatives.[17]

North American Aviation instituted far-reaching management changes, and NASA reexamined its associations with other contractors to better ensure safety procedures and quality control. The Grumman Corporation, for example, was instructed in mid-June to carefully inspect its lunar module to make certain that it was as safe as possible, paying particular attention to the possibility of a fire breaking out in the thin-skinned lunar landing vehicle. An eerie specter of *Apollo 1* was revisited just weeks later, in early July, when an Apollo lunar module burst into flames during tests at a NASA facility in New Mexico. But the craft was unmanned, and no one was hurt.

The *Apollo 1* Legacy

The loss of three men whose lives had been so intensely dedicated to the cause of space exploration forced NASA into an immediate, rigorous, and painful self-examination. And from the perspective of the long years since, the obvious conclusion arrived at by all those involved in the space agency at that time was that the only tragedy worse than having lost the crew of *Apollo 1* would be to have lost them in vain.

As a result, Grissom, White, and Chaffee were in many ways as responsible as anyone for the eventual landing on the moon. The changes wrought to the spacecraft as a result of their deaths were directly responsible for the safer passage of those who followed, and their tragic loss served as the horrific literal baptism of fire for Apollo, consecrating the program's commitment to the safety of its adventurers as a far greater priority than the objectives of the adventure itself.

No track in the lunar dust could ever compensate the wives, children, other family, and friends of those who were lost, but perhaps there was some small comfort in knowing that the journey to the moon could not have been made without the three men whose sacrifice resulted in vastly changed perceptions about the nature and purpose of space flight. Their loss forced everyone involved with the program to accept the very real possibility that the grand adventure could just as easily end in tragedy as in triumph. The fire was the ultimate reminder that no technological advance, political advantage, or national space goal—not even the moon itself—was worth more than a single human life. Whatever the specific objectives of any future mission, success would be measured first and foremost by the safety of the crew, and failure marked by the degree to which the astronauts came near to the sad fate of Grissom, White, and Chaffee. They would be present in every extra commitment to detail, each new choice that would in any way affect an astronaut's safety in the future. As the shadow of *Apollo 1* passed over the program, the crew's sacrifice would be felt in each new step toward the moon.[18]

Thus problems discovered in early May with the craft that would fly the first of the three newly planned, unmanned Apollo flights later in the year were addressed immediately by NASA and its contractors. Corroded plumbing, potentially disastrous holes in the capsule's heat shield, a balky timer, and more than a thousand minor electrical faults would be addressed before the spacecraft left the ground.

Apollos 4, 5, and *6*

In deference to the deceased crew, the next Apollo to fly was dubbed *Apollo 4*. It was launched atop a complete Saturn V stack on November 9, 1967, successfully testing the three-stage rocket's flight performance for the first time, and marking the initial flight in space of Apollo command and service modules. The command module reentered the earth's atmosphere at a speed of 25,000 miles per hour from a height of 10,000 feet, successfully simulating the return from the moon that future manned capsules would have to endure. The temperature inside the capsule during the blistering reentry remained a comfortable, controlled 70 degrees Fahrenheit.

Two more unmanned Apollos followed, the January 1968 launch of *Apollo 5*, which marked the first flight of the lunar module, and *Apollo 6*, launched in April 1968.[19]

Even as the new tests were conducted and the way was prepared for the resumption of manned flights, the influence of the lost astronauts was felt throughout the remainder of the Apollo program. In a real and lasting way, the three men who gave their lives in the effort to begin the Apollo program, to fly the first spacecraft in the series that would eventually land a human being on the moon, were at the very heart of the program's scathing self-examination, slow healing, and renewal, and eventual success at the foot of the lunar module ladder when Neil Armstrong touched down on the moon two and a half years later.

It seemed especially fitting when Armstrong and Buzz Aldrin, as part of their epoch-marking landing, and not knowing at the time if human beings would ever make it back for another visit, left behind on the surface of the moon five small tokens in remembrance of lost heroes. The small markers commemorated the lives and efforts of Gus Grissom, Ed White, Roger Chaffee, Vladimir Komarov, and Yuri Gagarin. Together they gave some small credence to the other, more famous plaque the astronauts left behind, which reads in part, "We came in peace for all mankind."

5

Apollo Before the Moon: Into The Light

The first Apollo to lift off with astronauts inside was *Apollo 7*, which launched on October 11, 1968. The space program's long "dark period," while the fire was being studied and the spacecraft was being redesigned, was coincidentally a time of upheaval and unrest for America.

In ironic parallel to the tragic fire and the searching reexamination that followed it at NASA, the nation at large suffered a period of public violence and anger, which in turn gave rise to an increasingly acrimonious debate about its future course. The nation's involvement in the Vietnam War was the proximate cause of many of the events that marked 1968 as a watershed year, and the U.S. presidential campaign was the catalyst that set many of those events in motion.

For their part, the astronauts continued to train for future missions during the twenty months between the loss of *Apollo 1* and the *Apollo 7* flight. The training would be necessary in any case, but the greater complexity of the planned landing on the moon added many hours to the already daunting training regimen. For example, the *Apollo 7* crew, preparing to test the redesigned spacecraft in earth orbit, spent some 600 hours rehearsing their flight in earthbound simulators, while the crew of *Apollo 11* spent 2,000 hours simulating their lunar landing mission.[1]

The particulars of upcoming missions remained up in the air while the men who would execute them stayed on the ground. But the need for the astronauts to become familiar with the Apollo vehicles and systems was crucial to the program's smooth operation once flights were resumed.

For the entirely new element of flying the lunar module, the thin-skinned, spindly-legged two-stage spaceship that would handle the last leg of the journey to the moon's surface, a similar craft was built for flying on earth. In keeping with the dictates of NASA-speak, the odd-shaped rig was dubbed the lunar landing training vehicle (LLTV).

Neil Armstrong was piloting the LLTV during an early May training exercise when it suddenly exploded, sending a plume of black smoke into the sky. Careful observers noted a flash of bright flame amid the dark veil, a welcome sign that Armstrong had managed to trigger the craft's ejection seat before the explosion could claim him. As the craft thudded to the ground, those observing the flight were relieved to pick out the orange and gray shades of the astronaut's parachute in the far distance. He floated back to earth at a safe distance from the burning wreckage of the ruined LLTV.

It was perhaps less dramatic than his previous close call, when he and Dave Scott were nearly killed by their malfunctioning *Gemini 8* capsule, but Armstrong's near-miss with the LLTV again proved his superior calm in life-and-death situations, and his superb instincts as a pilot.[2]

These were, of course, the skills for which he and the others had been selected, and for which they were so revered by the public. In the astronauts, America had heroes who could be embraced without reservation, as they represented achievement, courage, and skill by pushing the boundaries of their own abilities, challenging the physical limitations of being human. In doing so, they brought out the best in others.

America in Turmoil

Along with his "Great Society" social programs to aid the poor, Lyndon Johnson's support of America's progress in space during the difficult 1967–1968 period was indicative of the best instincts of his administration. Whatever the political debate over the means or methods employed by each of these efforts, or their ultimate value, the idealism with which they were pursued seems admirable even three decades later.

In stark contrast, the administration's conduct of the war in Vietnam caused it to become increasingly alienated from the American people. As the 1968 presidential campaign began in anticipation of the March New Hampshire primaries, Johnson faced the very real possibility that he might not be able to win the renomination of the Democratic party. A growing perception that the United States would ultimately fail to win even a negotiated standoff in Vietnam fueled an increasingly acrimonious debate about the war.

On January 30 and 31—at the start of the Tet holiday, during which the Vietnamese celebrate the start of the lunar new year—the Communist Viet Cong launched a major offensive. Troops surged into more than a hundred cities and towns throughout South Vietnam, and a small band of Communist guerrillas infiltrated the grounds of the U.S. embassy in the South Vietnamese capital, Saigon. For the first time, the war moved from rural battlefields to the South's urban strongholds.

American troops performed exceptionally well and reversed most of the North's advances (including their push into the courtyard of the American embassy, which lasted a little more than six hours). Scenes of the grim fighting and news of the bold nationwide attack were widely interpreted by the American news media, and by extension the American people, as a devastating setback for the United States and further evidence that the president was not being truthful about the nation's progress in the war.

Television coverage of the Tet offensive and subsequent gruesome events in Vietnam stunned American viewers. The three television networks were exerting an unprecedented influence on public opinion; the familiar anchors and correspondents of ABC, CBS, and NBC were a regular part of the nightly routine in a majority of American homes. Dramatic events frequently brought large numbers of television viewers together in front of their sets, and a series of remarkable, enduring images was burnished in the collective consciousness of the American people as the year unfolded.

President Johnson exited the election campaign in a startling, televised withdrawal on March 31.

In brief filmed excerpts from his final sermon, the Reverend Martin Luther King Jr. poignantly described his spiritual journey: "I have been to the mountaintop. I have seen the glory. I may not get there with you, but I want you to know that we as a people will get to the promised land." The great civil rights leader was assassinated the next day, April 4, 1968, in Memphis, Tennessee.

And at the end of a long day's campaign and following his victory in the Democratic primary in California, Robert Kennedy was shot by an assassin in the early morning hours of June 5. Coverage of the campaign became coverage of the shooting, and the nightmarish images of that evening are easily among the saddest and most horrifying in the history of broadcast journalism.

The assassination also set the stage for a bizarre confrontation on the streets of Chicago in August as antiwar protesters and the city's police force were embroiled in a long, savage confrontation outside the hall where the Democratic National Convention was taking place. While the Democrats inside chose Hubert Humphrey to face Republican candidate Richard Nixon in November, the violence outside was broadcast to the rest of the nation.

Apollo 7: **A Cautious Return**

Thus it was a weary America, frightened by images of violence and horror and saddened by a seemingly endless parade of bad news, that witnessed Apollo's return to the national stage in November of 1968. Even the program's detractors had to be careful about phrasing their reservations after the fire, out of respect for the three lost astronauts. And in contrast to virtually everything else that had made news throughout the year, the attempt to return to space seemed especially uplifting and noble.[3]

Apollo 7 would be the first American spacecraft to carry a three-man crew. Mercury veteran Wally Schirra commanded the mission, accompanied by group-three astronauts Walter Cunningham and Donn Eisele. Schirra became the first astronaut—and, as it subsequently turned out, the only one—to fly a mission during each of the Mercury, Gemini, and Apollo programs. That particular achievement did not hold a lot of joy for the veteran astronaut, however, as it would have been Gus Grissom's honor instead had he lived.

The *Apollo 1* fire had deeply affected Schirra. He announced in advance that *Apollo 7* would be his final flight in space, and he embarked on the mission with a full awareness of the importance of its success. Safety was the top priority, an absolute necessity in renewing public commitment to John Kennedy's dream of reaching the moon by the end of the decade—and indeed, of reaching the moon at all.[4]

A new appreciation of the astronauts' challenge began to filter into the public consciousness. Although the Soviets continued their push toward the moon during the same period, competition between the superpowers became a far less prevalent part of the media's coverage of the American program. There was certainly enough to talk about on the American side, as NASA and its astronauts geared up for the return to space, but there may also have been some element of residual guilt on the part of all those, in the media and in the public at large, who had hyped the space race to such a degree in the past. The question of how the nation's fervor for beating the Russians to the moon may have influenced the circumstances that led to the *Apollo 1* catastrophe was left largely unanswered, even after the exhaustive probe of the fire was complete.

The Soviet program followed a trajectory similar to NASA's for much of 1967 and 1968. In the wake of their own tragic loss, when Vladimir Komarov was killed in the *Soyuz 1* accident in April 1967, the Soviets carefully reexamined their equipment and systems and began to make modifications. Working with the basic Soyuz model, they were able to put together a moonship, the Zond, that they tested in unmanned flights throughout 1968. In September, *Zond 5* flew around the moon and returned to earth, splashing down in the Indian Ocean. Although it had no crew, the flight was a clear indicator of how close the USSR was to attempting a lunar landing.

In October the unmanned *Soyuz 2* lifted off, followed the next day by *Soyuz 3* with cosmonaut Georgi Beregovoi aboard, for a brief mission that tested rendezvous maneuvers. October also brought a change in the NASA hierarchy, when James Webb, who had headed the agency since 1961, was replaced by Dr. Thomas Paine.

Apollo 7 launched on October 11, 1968. The redesigned spacecraft worked well during its eleven days in earth orbit, much to the relief of the contractors who had built it, NASA's administrative and engineering personnel, and the nation as a whole, a good portion of which followed the astronauts' exploits thanks to the first extensive television coverage of a mission in progress.

Beyond the glare of public attention, however, a serious tension developed between the crew and officials directing the flight from the ground. Schirra openly expressed his disdain when asked to perform a series of tests that had not been part of the original flight plan, and the crew's contempt for mission control grew ever more obvious in the final few days before their return to earth.

Reentry preparations led to the most serious disagreement of all. Suffering from a severe cold, Schirra asked mission control for permission to reenter without his space helmet. He apparently feared that the pressure of the atmosphere could do permanent damage to his inner ear. Particularly concerned with the safety of the crew on this first manned mission after the fire, flight director Chris Kraft and the NASA medical staff in Houston strongly urged Schirra to follow the prescribed procedures of reentry to the letter, which included the wearing of one's helmet. Schirra, equally concerned with safety and seeing the problem from a decidedly different perspective, followed his own instincts.

It was a decision that had no adverse consequences. Schirra, Cunningham, and Eisele splashed down without incident, and but for the personality clashes with the ground, their mission was a stunning success. For all the difficulties with their recalcitrant commander, NASA had gotten an excellent farewell flight from Wally Schirra. At the same time, openly rebellious conduct could be neither tolerated nor encouraged; as such, the most lasting negative consequence of the *Apollo 7* flight affected Walter Cunningham and Donn Eisele, who were both denied the chance to fly again in space.[5]

First Around the Moon

The success of *Apollo 7* put the American space program back on track. It opened the way for the next steps in the carefully planned march to the moon, which were, as logic dictated, a full test of the joined Apollo command and lunar modules in earth orbit. That was the original profile for the *Apollo 8* mission.

Then, on November 10, the Soviets launched *Zond 6*, another unmanned lunar flyby that landed in Russia a week later, having traveled to the moon and back.

Certain that the Russians were close to a manned trip around the moon, NASA's highest officials considered changing the profile of the next Apollo mission, to put Americans in lunar orbit before the year's end. The proposal made sense for a variety of reasons beyond the need to beat the Soviets: it would thoroughly test the program's communications abilities at lunar distances, result in excellent close-up photos of potential lunar landing sites, and provide medical and systems data necessary for future flights. Perhaps most important, it would give a crew hands-on expertise in piloting an Apollo to the moon, without the added complexity of working with the lunar module, which was not yet ready.

For all its benefits, the decision to jump *Apollo 8* forward in the scheme of things meant that virtually any disaster that endangered the life of the crew could result in the end of the entire space program or, at the very least, a lengthy hiatus that would put the moon beyond reach of the end-of-the-decade deadline.[6]

In their book *Moon Shot*, Alan Shepard and Deke Slayton recount that James McDivitt, the Gemini veteran who had been selected as commander of *Apollo 8*, was offered the revised mission earlier in the year but turned it down. *Apollo 7* had not yet flown, and McDivitt and his crew were immersed in training for the original flight, which would be the first earth orbit test of the command and lunar modules. There was still a great amount of uncertainty about how the program would develop if there were problems with Schirra's *Apollo 7*, and at the time the likelihood of McDivitt's original mission seemed a much better bet than the possibility of anyone at NASA committing to a lunar mission that early.[7]

So McDivitt's flight became *Apollo 9*, when the crew originally scheduled for that mission—Frank Borman, Jim Lovell, and Bill Anders—agreed to move up in the rotation and take the new trip now aimed at the moon. As it turned out, both crews performed flawlessly, each bringing the United States a step closer to the epochal landing.

Apollo 8: Around the Moon

In its audacity, flying out into the heavens just as millions of Americans began their celebration of the 1968 Christmas holiday season, *Apollo 8* was "shooting the moon" in more ways than one. If the mission was successful, it would give Borman, Lovell, and Anders an unprecedented chance to communicate the space program's highest aims directly to a global audience of some 500 million television viewers back on earth. If something went wrong along the way, the crisis would be the last dark moment of an exceedingly dark year.

For all the science that preceded it, the voyage of the first spacecraft to bring human beings to the edge of the moon was a journey outside of time, an irreplaceable, ageless first close look at the mysterious orb that had haunted humanity since the dawn of civilization.

And for all it would say about its passage, *Apollo 8* would also give the American public new insight about the nature of the men who had trained so long and worked so hard for the chance to risk their lives in space. Television coverage of the flight testified to the astronauts' strength of character and their good-natured willingness to cooperate with each other in the small craft and with the massive team directing the effort from the ground.

Typical of the astronauts' best instincts at each end of the spectrum of emotional response was an exchange between Jim Lovell in the *Apollo 8* capsule and Michael Collins, who was monitoring the flight at mission control in Houston.

Lovell eloquently reflected on the earth from his unique perspective: "What I keep imagining is if I'm some lonely traveler from another planet, what I'd think of earth at this altitude . . . whether I'd think it would be inhabited or not."

"You don't see anybody waving, do you?" joked Collins in response.[8]

When they reached the moon, Borman, Lovell, and Anders expressed an almost religious awe at the sight of the lunar surface passing beneath their window. A vision of acute desolation emerged, a lonely landscape of dry craters and broken rocks on a dead world.

And then, suddenly, as *Apollo 8* moved farther along in its orbit, the sight of the bright earth just across the lunar horizon was a sort of cosmic punch line, a silent, joyous reminder that the long-ago-predetermined fate of the moon was not that of the earth. The astronauts' account of the warm color of the brilliant, live earth was authentic in the singular manner of the eyewitness, and in that one instant all the astronomy, the scientific photographs, the theories of the great thinkers and the poetic words of the great dreamers down through the ages were rendered irrevocably less authentic than the simple testimony streaming back through space from *Apollo 8*.

Celebrating Christmas Eve orbiting the moon, Anders, Lovell, and Borman took turns reading from the Bible. Anders began: "For all the people on earth, the crew of Apollo Eight has a message we would like to send you." And then he began reading from the Book of Genesis: "In the beginning, God created the heaven and the earth, and the earth was a formless wasteland, and darkness covered the abyss, while a mighty wind swept over the waters. Then God said, 'Let there be light, and there was light.' God saw how good the light was. God then separated the light from the darkness. God called the light 'day,' and the darkness he called 'night.' Thus evening came, and morning followed—the first day."

Anders read the first four verses of the Christian story of the world's beginning, then Lovell continued with the next four, and then Borman finished the reading. When he was done, the *Apollo 8* commander added a valedictory: "And from the crew of Apollo Eight, we close with good night, good luck, a Merry Christmas, and God bless all of you—all of you on the good earth."[9]

For a few brief moments, the *Apollo 8* crew had given voice to a higher purpose of space exploration, one that had meaning for every earthly individual who cared or worried or even occasionally thought about the nature of his or her own existence. The journey into space of one man or woman, or two or three or however many would ever make the trip, was significant not just for the physical document it could produce of the look or type or composition of the worlds floating around with the earth, but also for the feeling that only a witness can convey, in testimony that can give hope to a weary world.

Racing around the moon on their unprecedented flight, Borman, Lovell, and Anders revealed the light of the earth in a way that only a human being that far from home could. And in so doing, they gave the long ride a meaning that far surpassed the logic of those who decried the risks or cost of the endeavor, or who questioned the ultimate value of the trip.[10]

In America, the "Christmas Apollo" was a bright break in the long line of grim events that had made 1968 unique. War, assassination, violence, and political upheaval were finally given some small counterbalance, the good news that somewhere in the heavens humanity was moving forward in some way, even as the country seemed to be descending into madness. Perhaps the view from Apollo allowed a glimpse of better days to come.

1969: The New Year

The new year dawned bright for NASA, coming off the multiple successes of the *Apollo 7* and *Apollo 8* flights, back on track to reach the moon before year's end as long as everything continued to go as planned.

Still pushing their own way toward the moon, the Soviets launched *Soyuz 4* on January 14 with cosmonaut Vladimir Shatalov aboard, and sent *Soyuz 5* into space the next day with a three-man crew, Boris Volynov, Alexei Yeliseyev, and Yevgeni Khrunov. The two craft docked in earth orbit and swapped crew members from one craft to the other, leading the Soviets to proclaim that the joined craft were the "first experimental space station." While it did break some new ground and perhaps pointed the way toward later, more substantial Russian advances such as the *Mir* space station, the mission was largely dismissed as a Soviet attempt to gain attention at a time when the American program was getting closer and closer to the first lunar landing.[11]

A sense of cautious optimism had begun to emerge in the United States about the prospects for less tumultuous times and, in particular, about the prospects of an end to the Vietnam War. Promising to restore a sense of calm in the nation and claiming that he had a "secret plan" to end the war, Richard Nixon had defeated Democrat Hubert Humphrey in the fall, and was sworn in as president on January 20.

As Eisenhower's vice president during the crucial first phase of the space race, Nixon had advocated a more vigorous American space program; now he would have the honor of presiding over the first moon landing. For Nixon, there was a certain irony involved in that honor, as many Americans still associated the moon landing with John Kennedy, his polar opposite who had so narrowly defeated him during the 1960 campaign. But there were few politicians in the modern era who were so definitively associated with the ebb and flow of the great events of the day as Richard Nixon, and his enthusiasm for celebrating that particular moment was obvious.[12]

In February, the Soviets suffered another setback when a test of their powerful N-1 booster, the rocket that carried their hopes of reaching the moon, ended in a fiery explosion just a little more than a minute after launch. It was one in a series of misfires for the N-1, the net result of which would be the failure of the Soviet moon program.[13]

The next test for the American program would be to try out the lunar module, the last piece of the Apollo puzzle, in earth orbit. *Apollo 5* had been the first in the series to carry the moon craft, but that had been an unmanned mission with far more limited objectives. Now, with both the decade and the deadline of reaching the moon before its end running short, the lunar module would be carefully tested in earth orbit, and then again in lunar orbit, before the landing could take place.

Apollo 9: Testing the Lunar Module

Jim McDivitt was the commander of *Apollo 9*. The last time he had flown in space prior to this mission, McDivitt had carefully kept watch from inside *Gemini 4* while Ed White took his historic walk in space. That moment had been just four years earlier, but for all those who had known White as well as McDivitt had, the time prior to *Apollo 1* must have seemed much farther away.

Also on the *Apollo 9* crew were Dave Scott, on his first mission since his harrowing trip on *Gemini 8*, and group three astronaut Rusty Schweickart, flying into space for the first time.

The intervention of the "unplanned mission"—the lunar orbit flight of *Apollo 8*—had given the crew even more time to prepare for that moment when they finally lifted off, on March 3, 1969. Shortly afterward, testing the procedures that would be used on all later flights, the astronauts pulled their command module free of the spent rocket that had put them into orbit, then turned it around and locked it onto the lunar module, still encased in its protective covering within the Saturn. With another elegant maneuver, the joined command and lunar modules were free, flying together in space for the first time.

As with all the Apollo missions that carried a lunar landing craft, the need for separate call signs to identify the command and lunar modules gave the crew a chance to name the vehicles, frequently with the waggish humor that NASA had long ago deemed inappropriate for the nature of the tasks at hand. And given the appearance of the vehicles in question the names devised for the *Apollo 9* command and lunar modules seemed particularly apt: they were called *Gumdrop* and *Spider.*

Vigorous tests of the lunar module proved the weird-looking little craft worthy of the intentions of NASA's engineers. Along the way, Rusty Schweickart tested the portable life-support system (PLSS), the space suit that later astronauts would wear during their excursions on the lunar surface, during a half-hour extravehicular activity.

Halfway through the ten-day mission, McDivitt and Schweickart pulled the lunar module—*Spider*—away from *Gumdrop*, the command module, and flew the lunar craft on its first solo flight. They fired the descent engine of the two-stage craft, pushing themselves into a higher orbit than the command module and simulating the process that would take later astronauts to the lunar surface.

Once they had cleared the initial hurdle of maneuvering with the descent engine, McDivitt and Schweickart completed the test by jettisoning the descent stage entirely, firing the ascent engine to rendezvous with Scott in the command module, and then joining him for the return trip to earth.

Apollo 9 was a resounding success, splashing down in the Atlantic on March 13 with all its major objectives accomplished without incident.[14]

Anticipation of the first landing on the moon now grew. The question of which mission would be the first to touch down hinged on the speed with which the weight of the lunar module could be reduced; the model available for *Apollo 10*'s launch in May was too heavy to return to lunar orbit if it was used for a landing. Within NASA, there was some consideration of postponing the flight until a lighter craft was available; perhaps surprisingly, *Apollo 10* commander Tom Stafford was apparently one of those who argued in favor of the benefits of a complete rehearsal in lunar orbit. His crewmate Gene Cernan noted later that Stafford was less concerned with being first on the moon than he was with keeping the space program safely moving forward.[15]

Like McDivitt, who chose to continue training for his original mission rather than command the first Apollo to head for lunar orbit, Stafford decided to continue with the all-important tests of the communications, radar, guidance, and propulsion systems just above the surface of the moon, without the added risk and complexity of a landing. The validation those tests would provide would increase the odds of a safe first landing on the next mission, *Apollo 11*, in July.

Key to the NASA decision-making process at the time was administrator Thomas O. Paine, who had taken the agency's helm in March and would head it through the first landing.

So, for only the second time in history, a manned spacecraft would travel to the moon. Fellow space veteran John Young joined Stafford and Cernan on the flight. They lifted off on May 18, 1969.

Apollo 10: A Last Close Look

In the tradition of *Gumdrop* and *Spider*, the command and lunar modules of *Apollo 10* were known as *Charlie Brown* and *Snoopy*, in honor of the main characters of Charles Schulz's popular comic strip, *Peanuts.*

A few hours into the flight, the astronauts fired the third-stage engine of the Saturn V rocket that had boosted them into orbit, and headed for the moon. When they reached it, they passed around its far side and slipped into lunar orbit. A pleasant sense of relief permeated mission control as they emerged from the far-side communications blackout at precisely the expected instant, indicating that all had gone well.

As the mission progressed, Stafford and Cernan entered the lunar module, undocked from the command module, and maneuvered into an orbit that took them as close as 47,000 feet from the surface of the moon.

They tested the lunar module's radar system—the radar "eye" that would guide *Apollo 11* safely down to the dusty landscape—and carefully examined a potential backup site for the first landing. Further tests of the lunar module's descent engine followed as they moved to a new orbit, and on their next trip around, they passed directly over the spot where *Apollo 11* was scheduled to land two months later.

All that was left was a test of the procedures that would later be necessary for lifting off the surface and returning to the command module.

The first step of that phase of the mission was to jettison the descent stage of the lunar module. As they began the procedure, Stafford and Cernan felt a sudden jolt as the ascent stage fell into an uncontrolled spin. The two astronauts quickly ran through the nuts and bolts of the procedure and came across a switch that had been flipped in the wrong direction. Reflecting on the mishap later, Cernan guessed that in his eagerness to execute his portion of the maneuver, he had accidentally reached across the maze of controls and set the switch—which was on Stafford's side of the control panel and was his responsibility—to the desired position. As a result, when the commander ran through his part of the procedure, he inadvertently returned the switch to the improper setting.

It was a minor mistake, with little impact on the overall mission. Stafford had found and corrected the problem within eight seconds. But it was another reminder of the complex nature of spaceflight, and the ever-present dangers that could arise from even the simplest errors.[16]

Other than those scary eight seconds, the break from the descent stage and subsequent rendezvous with the command module went well, and after Stafford and Cernan had safely rejoined Young, they jettisoned the lunar module. Mission control fired the craft's engine a final time, sending it into orbit around the sun.

Despite the few minor difficulties that the crew faced over the course of their mission, *Apollo 10* produced plenty of encouraging proof that the spacecraft, systems, and expertise of the American program had progressed enough to make the planned landing a risk worth taking.

The sun was shining on *Snoopy*, *Charlie Brown* was safe at home, and Apollo was ready to step onto the moon and into the pages of history.

6

Apollo 11: Life on an Ancient World

The moon has been silent, austere, and alone from the moment of its creation. For billions of years it has danced alongside the earth, circling its tumultuous neighbor as that world grew and flourished and, eventually, brought forth a form of life that could itself transform into a tiny little satellite, move across the heavens, and drop in for a visit.

Curiosity about the moon—what it meant, and why by some cosmic logic it had been placed "up there" to rise each dark night and then hide every glaring day—had caused human beings to think, and to wonder, throughout their history on earth. The mysteries of the moon seemed new each time a child looked aloft for the first time and saw more than a simple silhouette in the sky, adorning the ethereal world with gentle myths and the romance of an innocent heart.

All the data the space program had gathered since the mid-1950s made it clear that humans landing on the moon would not likely face little green men, catastrophic changes in climate, or a terrain that would fall away beneath their feet. NASA had done its homework carefully, and eliminated as many risks as possible as it prepared to send the astronauts all the way to the lunar surface.

Thus the final preparations for *Apollo 11* took on an air of joyous

expectancy as Americans followed the space agency's progress and readied themselves to share in the event via television. The landing would
take place during the summer, when children throughout the country
would be enjoying a two-month break from school and many families
would be traveling on summer vacations, perhaps feeling a bit more
kinship with the astronauts in their ultimate journey.[1]

The Last Lap of the Space Race

For their part, the Soviets were in the lunar race to the last. They experienced another failure of the massive N-1 rocket in February, which in
effect cost them any chance of beating Apollo to the surface of the moon,
but on July 3 they tried again. Once more the temperamental booster
lifted off, and again it exploded before breaching the earth's atmosphere.
An escape tower saved the unmanned Soyuz spacecraft that sat atop the
launch stack, but the craft was of little use to the Soviet program without
a rocket that could reliably propel it into space.[2]

The fact that U.S. reconnaissance satellites quickly registered the force
of the N-1's fiery demise, which was akin to a nuclear blast in its explosive power, was a telling measure of just how far the cultivation of space
had advanced in a bit more than a decade. Only eleven years earlier, at
the dawn of the space race, there were no satellites peering downward or
massive rockets headed upward.

In that short time, the Russians had enjoyed a number of spectacular
space achievements, and in response, NASA had carefully prepared a
course to catch up and to seize the most impressive first of all. The
agency's creation, its growth, and now, in the summer of 1969, its crowning leap into history were defining elements of the American ethos in
the latter part of the twentieth century. A vast enterprise of corporate
teamwork, with its individuals' countless acts of self-sacrifice enmeshed
in the marrow of its bones, NASA's long reach of expertise and hard
work combined brilliant science and dreamy idealism, and that careful
mix proved a winning combination.

The simple premise of bridging the gap between the earth and moon
belied the vast complexity of NASA's task and its superb performance
during the moon flights. Certainly its heroes, the astronauts, were quick
to credit the collective brilliance of all the individuals who supported
their efforts.

Armstrong expressed the gratitude of the space flyers in typically
thoughtful fashion during the ride home from the lunar surface:

The inspiration for this flight lies first with history and with the giants of science who have preceded this effort. Next with the American people, who have, through their will, indicated their desire. Next to four administrations and their Congresses for implementing that will, and then to the agency and industry teams that built our spacecraft. We would like to give a special thanks to all those Americans who built those spacecraft, who did the construction, design, the tests and put their hearts and all their abilities into the craft.[3]

There is no small poetry in envisioning each grain of lunar dust in the astronauts' boot imprints on the moon as the symbolic relic of some small sacrifice on the part of their families, friends, and coworkers throughout the vast enterprise of the American space effort. In their own way, each of those individuals went along with the crew of *Apollo 11* and shared that first step onto the lunar surface in a way that others cannot fully understand or appreciate.

The First Three Days

The epic journey began at 9:32 a.m. EST on July 16, 1969. The all-veteran crew of commander Neil Armstrong, lunar module pilot Buzz Aldrin, and command pilot Michael Collins lifted off atop the stately Saturn V, playing out the first few notes of an ancient lyric dream. Watching on television in unprecedented numbers, ordinary citizens across the nation wondered in awe at the mighty rocket spewing flames, catapulting the tiny spacecraft into the heavens. After years of racing the Russians into space, surviving the death of the president who had inspired the trip, the loss of the *Apollo 1* crew, and the long descent into Vietnam that etched the dark side of the American spirit as fully as Apollo illuminated its bright face, the nation was finally going to the moon.

The launch and the trip out of the earth's atmosphere went smoothly. Once they were in space, just three hours after liftoff, Collins directed the command module *Columbia* into the separation maneuver, then swung the craft around in search of the lunar module (LM) *Eagle*. The LM loomed awkwardly in the darkness of the Saturn's third stage, the rim of the spent rocket forming a sort of halo around it as Collins reached in with *Columbia*'s probe to pull the spindly craft loose. The docking procedure was flawless, and the trip continued without incident.[4]

Three days passed during the 238,000-mile first leg of the journey. The crew slipped into lunar orbit on July 19, only the third group of human beings ever to do so, and Armstrong and Aldrin prepared to leave Collins and ride down to the surface.

The *Eagle* Flies

Having experienced the proximate sensations thousands of times in simulators back home, the crew had obviously had some time along the way to reflect on the nature of their undertaking, and their understanding of the mission's import punctuated the official communications. Thus when the command and lunar modules separated, Armstrong exclaimed, "The Eagle has wings!"

Estimates vary, but as many as one billion people are believed to have seen some portion of the *Apollo 11* television coverage. The world watched and waited as Armstrong and Aldrin maneuvered the *Eagle* toward the surface of the moon.[5]

As the craft slid through the lunar sky, gliding ever closer to its unprecedented landing, the long journey's first tense bit of drama popped up, in the form of a flashing warning light glaring outward from the control console of the lunar module.

"Twelve-oh-two," Aldrin said simply, identifying the warning light. At 33,500 feet above the lunar surface, the LM was just minutes away from touchdown.[6]

Controllers on the ground identified the problem immediately: the onboard computer was overloaded with data streaming in from the landing radar. Just as quickly, the engineers in Houston determined that the degree to which the computer was overwhelmed was not extreme enough to abort the landing. A chorus of affirmatives rang out as flight director Gene Kranz polled the staff tracking the flight; the key go came from guidance officer Stephen G. Bales, the controller responsible for monitoring the LM's computer activity. In the very short time he had to determine *Eagle*'s fate, based on training, simulation, and sheer gut instinct, he grasped the extent of the problem and determined that it would not force the crew to pull back. The good word was flashed to capsule communicator ("capcom," in NASA lingo) Charlie Duke, who then relayed it to his relieved fellow astronauts a quarter million miles away.

A few minutes later, even closer to touchdown, Bales faced the choice again when another alarm rang out. Again he saw the problem in perspective, and declared its scope insufficient to stop *Eagle*'s progress.

Bales's courageous split-second call earned him a place in the NASA pantheon, and made him a fitting exemplar of the quiet expertise that permeated the agency. It would also earn him a similar honor, as he later joined the three *Apollo 11* astronauts in receiving the Medal of Freedom from President Nixon.[7]

With mission control's blessing, Armstrong and Aldrin continued their descent to the surface. At about five hundred feet Armstrong grasped the pistol grip of the attitude controller assembly, a joysticklike device that allowed him to maneuver the craft the last bit of the way down. He looked out at the lunar landscape to find a sea of craters alongside a field of boulders—neither hospitable to landing—even as the LM dropped lower and the seconds before impact dwindled to a precious few. Armstrong made a last-minute adjustment to the spaceship's course, maneuvering it toward an open spot amid the lunar debris.

"Sixty seconds," Duke advised them from Houston, indicating that they had sixty seconds of fuel left.

Aldrin called out the particulars of the movement, as he had since the descent began: "Two and a half down . . . four forward . . . drifting to the right a little . . ."

And then they were on the surface of the moon, landed in the area known as the Sea of Tranquility.

"Okay. Engine stop," Aldrin finished the technical narrative of the landing, and Duke marked the moment in Houston: "We copy you down, *Eagle*."[8]

The exact instant came at 4:17:42 p.m. Eastern daylight time, July 20, 1969. Through the emanations of two tiny, fragile sparks of life borrowed momentarily from its brighter, livelier companion, the silent world spoke for the first time.

Suddenly, unforgettably, Armstrong's voice rang out across the vast ocean of space. "Houston, Tranquility Base here. The Eagle has landed."

The First Step

Armstrong and Aldrin had little time for reflection. They immediately launched into procedures for liftoff, in case the lunar ground proved unable to support the LM. The initial stay-no stay decision came shortly after the landing, indicating that they were cleared by mission control to remain on the surface. Another stay decision followed shortly thereafter, and from that point forward it was obvious to everyone involved that the landing had been a success. Following a rest period, the next move would be *the* step, the first time in history that a human being would walk on the surface of the moon.

But first the astronauts had to pause to eat. To honor the religious aspects of the experience, Aldrin retrieved a small package of wine, a chalice, and a wafer of bread from his "personal preference kit," the tiny pack each astronaut used to take along small items of his own choosing, and celebrated communion. He preceded the ancient ritual with a short plea that appropriately summed up the moment, asking for a few moments of silence and inviting "each person listening in, wherever or whoever he may be, to contemplate for a moment the events of the last few hours and to give thanks in his own individual way."[9]

Following their meal, some four hours passed while Armstrong and Aldrin finished their preparations for leaving the LM. Then, seven hours after they'd first set down on the lunar terrain, they opened *Eagle*'s hatch and Armstrong began to move down the ladder of the craft in his bulky space suit, the hefty portable life-support system (PLSS) clinging like a tortoise's shell on his back. The combined weight of the astronaut and the suit and all its accoutrements approached 380 earth pounds, but in the lunar gravity, which is only one-sixth of earth's, that weight was magically transformed to about 60 pounds.[10]

Still looking inward at Aldrin, Armstrong stood on the tiny porch of the LM and began a slow, deliberate move to the edge. He hesitated a moment, responding to mission control's reminder to activate the television cameras before going any further. Then he was on the ladder, slowly backing down, still facing the LM as he carefully negotiated the steps.

When he hit the bottom, standing for a moment on the fat, flat, round footpad of the leg of the LM, he cautiously jumped back up to the lowest rung of the ladder. "It takes a pretty good little jump," he reported. Then he lingered a moment, extending the age of the distant moon a respectful instant further.

"I'm at the foot of the ladder." Finally, looking directly at the surface he was about to meet, Armstrong described it for mission control and the massive television audience, referring to the lunar module in affectionate shorthand: "The lem footpads are only depressed in the surface about one or two inches, although the surface appears to be very, very fine-grained as you get close to it. It's almost like a powder." Another pause, and then: "I'm going to step off the lem now."

Neil Armstrong stepped onto the moon and into history at 10:56 p.m. with the words "That's one small step for man, one giant leap for mankind."

He moved around alongside the lunar module with ease, to the relief of all those watching from earth, and scooped up a small sample of lunar rock with the long-handled "contingency sample collector," just in case an emergency forced a premature departure. But the mission remained remarkably trouble-free.

Aldrin followed within fifteen minutes. A brief exchange between the two men revealed something of their personalities. Looking around the airless, cloudless little world, at the ancient rocks and empty craters and the way the moon's horizon curved away at either end, rather than appearing flat like the much larger earth's, Armstrong marveled, "Isn't that something? Magnificent sight out here." Equally awed by the experience, Aldrin gave an almost poetic reply: "Magnificent desolation."

Working on the Moon

True to form and according to plan, the astronauts worked feverishly for most of the two hours and thirty-one minutes they were on the moon. They deployed several experiments, including a collector to gauge the solar wind, a seismometer to record meteoroid impacts on the moon and geological movements within it, and a laser reflector with a hundred prisms that would allow scientists to measure—among other things—the distance between the earth and moon to within just six inches, by directing an earth-based laser at the moon-based reflector.

There were other duties as well. An American flag was posted on a makeshift staff, driven into the surprisingly resistant surface with great effort, and Armstrong photographed Aldrin saluting it. Like the photographer of the family who records everyone else's vacation from behind the lens, the Apollo commander is absent from virtually all of the still photos of the astronauts working on the moon; Aldrin clicked a number of exposures of Armstrong, but all the images released by NASA following the mission were of Aldrin, by Armstrong.

In the spirit of international cooperation, a small metal plate inscribed with the goodwill wishes of seventy-three nations was also left alongside the American flag, as well as an *Apollo 1* patch in memory of Gus Grissom, Ed White, and Roger Chaffee, and medallions honoring the efforts of cosmonauts Vladimir Komarov and Yuri Gagarin.

Once the flag was in place, the astronauts received a decidedly long-distance congratulatory call from President Nixon. After a warm but brief conversation, they returned to their duties, unveiling along the way the plaque they would leave behind on the leg of the lunar module. It pictures the hemispheres of the earth, and features the signatures of each of the astronauts and the president, with the simple inscription "Here men from the planet Earth first set foot on the Moon. We came in peace for all mankind. July 1969 A.D."

And the work went on. Armstrong began to fill the sample collection boxes with lunar rocks, while Aldrin struggled to carve a core sample out of the lunar ground. As their time on the moon ran down, they worked together to load the LM with the precious boxes of moon rocks, Armstrong attaching them to the end of a pulley system that Aldrin then maneuvered to pull them on board. They had collected forty-six pounds of carefully selected specimens of lunar rock, eventually to be divvied up by some 150 laboratories back on earth, all eagerly awaiting their chance to study the unique samples.

Once the rocks were inside the lunar module, Armstrong took a last look and then bounded up the ladder. After a fitful night's rest, the lunar explorers would lift off, rendezvous with Collins and *Columbia*, and begin the long trip home.[11]

An Unexpected Visitor

Armstrong and Aldrin were not alone during their night on the moon. In addition to Collins circling overhead, keeping a lonely vigil in *Columbia*, there was a third craft nearby. *Luna 15*, launched by the Soviets three days before *Apollo 11* began its journey, had circled the moon more than fifty times during the previous four days.

The craft was apparently designed to make a soft landing, scoop up some samples of the lunar soil, and then race back to earth ahead of the *Apollo 11* crew, to steal some prestige from the American effort.

But *Apollo 11* seemed destined to succeed from the start. The mission progressed as though a part of nature, propelled by some unseen moral force inextricably enmeshed in the dreamlike quality it projected to the world watching from afar. There would be no asterisk attached to the *Apollo 11* achievement, no gadfly claim of a first sampling of lunar soil to nibble away at the accomplishment of the first landing.

As Armstrong and Aldrin slept on the surface of the moon and Collins slumbered above, *Luna 15* fired its engines and began its descent. Something quickly went wrong, and minutes later—at a speed of six hundred miles per hour—the little visitor crashed, poignantly enough, into the area of the moon known as the Sea of Crises.

Although the Soviets refused to provide any details about the flight, the Americans had closely tracked its progress. Mission control was able to record its fiery end with some precision, however; the violent crash registered prodigiously on the seismometer that Armstrong and Aldrin had left on the surface.[12]

It was a not altogether inappropriate reminder of the past, the space race, and the triumph and loss that had preceded *Apollo 11*'s epic flight. The incident also served as yet another reminder of the dangers that had been overcome by Armstrong, Aldrin, and Collins, and, by extension, all the others who had or would yet take up the career of flying in space. And in the final analysis, the failure of *Luna 15* proved the antithesis of what the Soviets would have likely claimed had it succeeded: that human beings were not necessary for space exploration. The three men sleeping on and around the moon were living proof that no machine could match the human mind and heart and spirit when it came to exploring the unknown. For all the data, the samples, and the technology, the most important element of human exploration was still the experience of the explorer himself.

Ascent and Return to *Columbia*

After twenty-one hours on the moon, Armstrong fired the engine of *Eagle*'s ascent stage, and he and Aldrin lifted off for the three-and-a-half-hour trip back to Collins and *Columbia*. The ascent stage shot upward at a rate of eighty feet per second, flawlessly propelling the astronauts away from the lunar surface. The sixteen-ton lunar module had performed exceptionally well on its first landing mission.

Floating in a higher orbit, Collins captured the return of the LM on film. Looking out *Columbia*'s tiny window, Collins could first see the little speck of a spacecraft against the wide expanse of the gray lunar landscape that filled his view. Then as it moved closer, it became identifiable as the craft whose appearance he had so carefully studied before the flight began.[13]

To ensure that he would know what the LM was supposed to look like when he saw it fully deployed prior to the landing, so he could alert his crewmates and mission control if anything seemed amiss, Collins had arranged a special visit to the factory where the manufacturer, Grumman Aircraft Engineering, had assembled it. It was yet another example of a small sacrifice of time and energy that helped to make sure that everything went exactly as planned during the flight.[14]

Now, on the return from the surface, it didn't make any difference what the LM ascent stage looked like, as long as it was intact and its inhabitants were okay. Radio contact had already confirmed that all was well, and as the final moments before the rendezvous slipped by, the LM was maneuvered into position for docking. The craft sent out a tiny point of reflected light like the pop of a camera's flashbulb as the bare plate with the big round hole in the middle was pushed around to face *Columbia*, and then *Eagle* was ready for its final duty before discharging the astronauts and their treasured samples.[15]

The docking was smooth, and after shaking the moon dust off their spacesuits, Armstrong and Aldrin rejoined Collins in the command module. The *Eagle* ascent module was left in lunar orbit, unlike all of its successors, which were sent back to the surface to deliberately crash-land, so their impact could be recorded by the instruments left behind on the lunar surface.

The Trip Home

Three more days passed until *Columbia* streaked out of the darkness of the early morning sky over the Pacific, its torrential descent at 25,000 miles per hour spewing balls of flame in an eerie, silent display of fireworks. In the water, the capsule flopped over on its side for a moment, and then righted itself according to plan, regaining a stately elegance even as it bobbed in the ocean.

Floating nearby, at the rail of one of the recovery ships, President Nixon smiled broadly and waved spontaneously with obvious, unrestrained joy.

Worries about the possibility of contamination by, as the media put it, "moon germs" forced the crew into a lengthy quarantine of twenty-one days. They donned special airtight suits before boarding the primary recovery ship, the USS *Hornet*, and immediately entered a specially designed van that could be hoisted off the ship and flown from one location to another, facilitating their return to mission control even while they were still cut off from the outside world.

The quarantine arrangement had an almost comic aspect to it, as the astronauts peered out and the world, via television, peered in. Their communications abilities were embodied in bright red phones with oversized handsets, a far cry in style and substance from the state-of-the-art equipment that they had been so carefully trained to use during their space flight and with which they had kept in touch with the earth from nearly a quarter of a million miles away.

Despite the precautionary quarantine, they had returned in excellent health. Collins looked a bit older, thanks to the mustache he'd sprouted; the first glimpse of the previously boyish-looking astronaut through the quarantine window was a bit jarring. But they were all well and in good spirits. When the involuntary medical hiatus ended, they began a worldwide whirlwind of promotional appearances that would change each of their lives in serious fashion. Generally private, serious-minded men used to piloting exotic airplanes and laboring over the details of rigorous training, they were largely unprepared for the seemingly endless requests for appearances, speeches, interviews, and promotional efforts that followed their *Apollo 11* triumph. In the spirit of that achievement, however, they continued to display good humor and patience to a remarkable degree.[16]

"The Greatest Week"

In those first few moments back on earth, however, the smiles came easily. The astronauts received the president through the large glass window of their quarantine cell, and he joked informally with them before delivering some prepared remarks.

"It is the spirit of Apollo that America can now help to bring to our relations with other nations," Nixon said, speaking with obvious emotion. "The spirit of Apollo transcends geographical barriers and political differences. It can bring the people of the world together in peace."[17]

Given the situation in Vietnam and the serious wave of national unrest about the conduct of the war, the president's comment about peace seemed incongruous at best, or even disingenuous or insincere. But in reality, the moon landing had freed him, if even for a short time, from the daily warfare of politics at home and abroad.

Years later, in his memoirs, Nixon himself seemed amazed at how caught up he had become in the spirit of the moment. After recounting his comment that the *Apollo 11* mission marked "the greatest week in the history of the world since the Creation," Nixon self-deprecatingly recalled the Reverend Billy Graham's comment that he had been "a little excessive" in his characterization.[18]

That tendency toward easy wit had come far more naturally to John Kennedy when he'd faced Nixon years before, in the 1960 presidential campaign. That election seemed very distant by the time of the moon landing. Nixon had brilliantly reinvented himself after his loss to Kennedy and his subsequent defeat in the California governor's race in 1962. He had created a "new Nixon" in the intervening years, and as he stood on the deck of the USS *Hornet* alongside the crew of *Apollo 11*, he looked like a new man, pleasant and happy and speaking earnestly of peace.

Richard Nixon welcomed the returning crew; Lyndon Johnson had nurtured the program through its worst days. But for many who felt something was irretrievably missing from the national political scene, who still mourned a young, vibrant president whose fascination had started it all, the *Apollo 11* moment was indelibly associated with the legacy of John F. Kennedy.

It had been his challenge to the American people, and his courage in the face of Soviet superiority, that had committed the United States to the course that was now finally, elegantly complete. NASA had met the president's challenge, landed men on the moon before the decade's end, and, most important, returned them safely to the earth.

In all that it said about the human spirit, and all it meant to those who understood it as having a meaning larger than science or technology or national pride alone, the first moon landing came to represent something inexpressibly personal.

At the same time, it was the high-water mark of American achievement in an era that also witnessed a wasteful foreign war and enormous division, anger, and bitterness throughout the nation. It gave the country's incumbent president an opportunity to demonstrate the buoyant humanity that was the essence of his potential for greatness; it gifted his predecessor with some measure of vindication for his progressive support of the program even as the ongoing war in Vietnam marred his legacy; and it powerfully demonstrated the lasting impact of the president whose spoken dream had stretched beyond his own days to become reality.

7

Apollo 12 and *Apollo 13*: Storms in Space

The tranquility of *Apollo 11* permeated the summer of 1969. In August the news media reported on the Woodstock festival, the three-day celebration of "peace, love, and rock and roll" that attracted a half million people to a farm in upstate New York. Linked by some to the cosmic significance of the moon landing, the peaceful cooperation of the overflow Woodstock crowd was cited as evidence of a new generosity of spirit.

There was a certain wry humor to the idea. The charm of Woodstock was at least as much a result of its collapse into utopian disarray amid the muddy fields as the success of *Apollo 11* was based on the astronauts' carefully planned mechanical precision among the craters of the moon. Even so, the choice of the two events as exemplars of a new attitude of peaceful cooperation was admirable and harmless, particularly in contrast to the ongoing flow of bad news about the progress of the war in Vietnam.

By November, though, the brief respite of summer had ebbed, and new tumults were about to descend across the nation. Through no fault of its own, *Apollo 12* started its long trip to the moon as an ironically appropriate symbol of the change in mood that was subtly altering the nation's psychic landscape.

Apollo 12: Sailing the Ocean of Storms

Apollo 12 reunited veterans Pete Conrad and Dick Gordon (they had flown together on *Gemini 11* in September 1966) and gave Alan Bean the chance to fly in space for the first time. All three had come to the space program from the U.S. Navy, and they had given their command and lunar modules nautical call signs in honor of their branch of the service. The command module, which would be piloted by Gordon, had been dubbed *Yankee Clipper*, and the lunar module (LM) would be known as *Intrepid.*

As Conrad, Gordon, and Bean waited atop the huge rocket assembly on November 14, 1969, heavy cloud cover and steady rain threatened to postpone their planned launch. Ironically enough, they were headed for the area of the moon known as the Ocean of Storms.

Because there was no lightning apparent among the clouds, the rainy launch was okayed, and the Saturn V began its task of thrusting the Apollo capsule skyward. A little more than a half a minute later, before the rocket had even cleared the skeletal infrastructure of the launch tower assembly, lightning lashed out of the murky sky.

Within the tiny Apollo capsule, the sudden pyrotechnics caused a serious power failure, plunging the crew into darkness. The ship's main circuit breakers had been triggered, temporarily cutting out its electric system. But the capsule's battery-operated backup electrical scheme automatically restored the craft's lights and instruments, and the Saturn V continued to fire, its separate guidance system unaffected by the lightning strike.

Both instances of saving grace were direct results of the ingenuity of NASA engineers. Layers of redundancy had been built into the design of virtually every major Apollo system for just this sort of unexpected emergency; thus the battery system kicked in until the circuit breakers could be reset. And the installation of separate control and guidance systems for the Saturn V and the Apollo capsule had been undertaken at the insistence of the engineering staff at the George C. Marshall Space Flight Center in Huntsville, Alabama.

With ninety-one engines and more than five and a half million parts, the fully assembled Apollo–Saturn V stack presented an enormously complex reliability challenge for the engineering teams responsible for its performance. As director of the Marshall Center and because of his high profile with Congress and the U.S. public, Wernher von Braun frequently addressed questions regarding the Apollo systems and equipment. In an interview published just prior to the moon landing in 1969, he explained the program's approach to reliability: "It's a matter of making every possible human effort to avoid a failure in a part," he said, "and then taking steps to avoid the effects of a failure if one should develop anyway."[1]

During *Apollo 12*'s first anxious moments, Conrad succinctly put the situation in perspective when he informed controllers on the ground about the scope of the instrumentation loss: "We just had everything in the world drop out." A bewildering array of warning lights came on all at once in the tiny capsule. For the moment, the good news was that the crew was fine. The condition of the spacecraft was less certain at first, but when Gordon reset the circuit breakers, the main electrical system responded immediately.

Even with the control and guidance systems again functioning properly, the entire complex of onboard computer programs had to be fed new code and validated within the spacecraft and on the ground. Working closely and as fast as possible given the scope of the problem, mission control and the crew were able to quickly refocus the electronic brains of the craft, and *Apollo 12* resumed its course toward the moon.[2]

A Smoother Ride

Things calmed down substantially after the shaky start. On November 19 Conrad and Bean traveled down to the moon's surface in *Intrepid*, achieving a particularly important goal by landing precisely in their preappointed target area, far west of the *Apollo 11* site. The *Surveyor 3* probe that had touched down on the lunar landscape two and a half years earlier, in April 1967, provided a familiar landmark nearby, confirming the accuracy of Conrad's skill in piloting the LM.

Passing overhead during his second orbit after the landing, Dick Gordon was able to view *Intrepid* and *Surveyor 3* on the lunar surface. It was an exciting moment for Gordon; four months earlier, a lack of precise data about where the *Apollo 11* LM had landed had prevented Michael Collins from seeing *Eagle* on the moon.[3]

Following the routine set by Armstrong and Aldrin, the crew on the surface ran through their preparations for walking on the moon. Unlike their predecessors, though, Conrad and Bean were free of the unique pressures of being the first to land. The weight of history was far less pressing for the third and fourth astronauts to walk on the moon, and the difference was reflected in the obviously relaxed way in which they interacted with each other and with mission control.

An early example took place when Conrad, at five feet six inches tall the most diminutive of all the Apollo astronauts, made the leap from the bottom of *Intrepid*'s ladder to the lunar surface. Recalling the gravity of Neil Armstrong's comment in the same situation a few months earlier, Conrad exclaimed, "Man, that may have been a small one for Neil, but that's a long one for me."[4]

A damaged television camera prevented the public from tagging along with the astronauts during their two extravehicular activities (EVAs), which was particularly frustrating in light of the obvious pleasure Conrad and Bean took in everything they did while on the surface. They deployed a number of experiments similar to but more advanced than those on *Apollo 11*, and collected seventy-five pounds of lunar rocks.

A Step into the Past

Most fascinating of all, they visited the *Surveyor 3* lunar probe, which had helped pave the way for the Apollo program years earlier. Ground controllers monitoring the landing of the unmanned probe had suspected that a stuck thruster had caused the craft to bounce around several times before it set down. Now, nearly two and a half years later, Conrad and Bean were able to confirm the precarious landing, thanks to several densely packed round "padprints" in the lunar dust, each just inches from *Surveyor 3*'s footpads.

They also removed *Surveyor*'s camera and several other pieces of the probe, to be brought back to earth so scientists could study the effect that a prolonged stay on the lunar surface would have on materials and equipment manufactured on earth.

The returned pieces of *Surveyor 3* injected an unexpected element of drama into the *Apollo 12* legacy when a microscopic biological organism was found on them following their return to earth. In sharp contrast to extreme interpretations that some sort of lunar life form had been discovered, scientists were in reality perplexed by the possibility that some sort of earthly organism had somehow survived the long trek to the moon and the long stay there. Subsequently, however, it was determined that the most likely explanation was that the samples had been inadvertently contaminated by the *Apollo 12* crew during their return flight.[5]

During their two trips outside the LM, Conrad and Bean spent a total of seven hours and forty-five minutes on the lunar surface. While they worked, deploying experiments, visiting *Surveyor 3*, and examining and collecting rock samples, they bantered back and forth with obvious enjoyment, and when the time came to seal up *Intrepid* and liftoff, they seemed reluctant to leave. Their visit had obviously been pleasant and, but for the loss of the television camera, certainly productive.

Ten days after their nerve-wracking launch, the crew of *Apollo 12* returned to earth, *Yankee Clipper* splashing down in the Pacific on November 24. Conrad, Gordon, and Bean had returned safe and in good spirits, with a sizable cache of moon materials to be studied, and NASA had an especially large number of blessings to count during the 1969 Thanksgiving holiday.

Problems loomed ahead. In January 1970, as the new decade dawned and the national commitment to the moon landings began already to recede into the windings of history, critics of the Apollo project redoubled their efforts to curtail or eliminate future missions. Following the massive attention focused on the first landing, public interest inevitably waned somewhat, and congressional support for the expensive moon program wavered in the face of political opposition. The original schedule of eight more missions was trimmed to seven; there would be no *Apollo 20.*[6]

The space agency's immediate concern, however, was the flight of *Apollo 13*, scheduled for April 1970. *Apollo 13* was unique in the program's history for the way in which its personnel shifted prior to launch day. The flight had originally been assigned to Alan Shepard, who had won his battle for reinstatement to flight status after overcoming the inner-ear problem that had kept him grounded for years, since he'd taken America's first ride into space back in 1961. A moon landing would certainly be a nice bookend accomplishment for America's first space hero, and Shepard himself was anxious to make the trip.

A walk in the lunar dust was also seen as a fitting culmination to the space travel career of Jim Lovell. As a member of the backup crew for *Apollo 11*, Lovell was expected to command *Apollo 14*, scheduled for launch some six months after *Apollo 13*. By now a familiar face in the space program thanks to his two Gemini missions and the *Apollo 8* lunar orbit trek, Lovell's experience and Shepard's need for additional training time with his crew led to the two missions being switched, with Lovell, Ken Mattingly, and Fred Haise moving up to take the *Apollo 13* assignment.

As though the wholesale changes in personnel weren't disruptive enough, Mattingly was then forced to give up his spot on the flight because the space agency's medical staff worried about his exposure to German measles seven days before launch. Fellow astronaut Charlie Duke, a member of the backup crew, had come down with the illness and unwittingly exposed the primary crew, and while Lovell and Haise had immunity through prior exposure, Mattingly did not. He was replaced by his backup, Jack Swigert, just days before the mission was set to begin.[7]

Mattingly, Swigert, and Haise were all group five astronauts, originally selected in April 1966, about six months before Lovell flew his second Gemini mission. For *Apollo 13*, Lovell and Haise had been chosen to visit the moon in the lunar module *Aquarius*, and in the revised lineup, Swigert would take Mattingly's place as pilot of the command module *Odyssey*.[8]

Apollo 13: The Longest Week

Apollo 13 lifted off on April 11, 1970, and experienced few problems during the first two-thirds of its three-day trek to the moon. The crew seemed relaxed and happy during their television broadcast, beamed back to mission control in the early evening of April 13.

Afterward, the astronauts ran through a series of routine tasks, including one known in the technojargon as a "cryo stir," or stirring of the service module's four cryogenic tanks, two of which contained oxygen and two that were filled with hydrogen. Occasionally thrashing around the contents was a necessity to ensure that their internal measuring devices produced accurate readings. The tanks themselves were crucial components of the flight, providing oxygen for the crew to breathe and a mix of oxygen and nitrogen to feed the three fuel cells supplying the spacecraft's electricity and water.

A sharp banging jolt resonated throughout the joined *Apollo 13* command, service, and lunar modules shortly after the cryo stir was completed. Within a few seconds, the crew and ground controllers at mission control were awash in a sea of warning lights, indicating that something had gone seriously wrong with the spacecraft.

"Hey, we've got a problem here," Swigert said as the craft shuddered from side to side.

"This is Houston, say again, please," replied astronaut Jack Lousma, the current capsule communicator in mission control.

"Houston, we've had a problem," Lovell confirmed. The veteran commander knew that the bang and ongoing vibration of the craft did not bode well.[9]

As the staff at mission control struggled to determine the nature of the incident and checked to see if the nightmarish glow of alarm lights could possibly be tracked to faulty instrumentation, the crew's first thoughts were of the possibility that a meteor had struck them. Haise rushed to the instrument panel to investigate while Lovell and Swigert struggled to close the hatch of the tunnel that separated the command module and lunar module. Their initial fear, that a meteor might have breached the fragile walls of the landing craft, exposing the entire assembly to the vacuum of space, proved unfounded.[10]

Whatever the cause of the trouble, a quick look out the window of the command module confirmed that something serious had taken place. From his now-precarious vantage point some 200,000 miles away from earth, Lovell radioed the bad news back to Houston: "It looks to me that we are venting something. We are venting something into space." The combination of instrument readings and Lovell's observation confirmed two things with absolute certainty: *Apollo 13* would not land on the moon, and the trip back to earth would not be an easy one.[11]

The Lifeboat

The astronauts' preliminary inspection of the inside of their spacecraft revealed that the lunar module was intact, but the command module was quickly losing the last of the electrical power it would need to fire its engine and bring the crew back to earth. The crew and mission control hit upon the best-case scenario at about the same moment; the astronauts' only hope of survival required the use of the lunar module as a sort of lifeboat.

For the rest of the trip through space, Lovell, Haise, and Swigert could draw life-sustaining oxygen from the lunar module and use its computer and propulsion systems for navigation and any necessary course corrections along the way. Although it could not withstand the heat and fire of reentry into the earth's atmosphere, *Aquarius* might at least keep the astronauts safe long enough for everyone to figure out how to revive the wasted command module.

First, though, *Odyssey* had to be shut down and *Aquarius* powered up. Swigert handled the first chore, carefully putting the command module into a sort of "deep sleep" mode, turning off everything in it that drew power while at the same time leaving it in a state from which, everyone hoped, it could be restored later on.

At the same time, Lovell and Haise prepared the lunar module to support the crew of three for what would likely be four more days in space. The LM had originally been intended to support the two astronauts during their trip to the lunar surface, during which it was expected to operate for a total of about forty hours.[12]

As risky as the situation was, there were no other options. *Apollo 13* was alone in space, hours away from the moon and days away from earth, and the survival of its crew depended entirely upon the ability of the lunar module to sustain them during the long trip home and the command module's ability to protect them from the harsh plummet through the atmosphere once they got there.

The timing of the accident had in a curious way been fortunate, coming as it did before the attempted landing. Generally the first few moments of any launch were the most dangerous, with the massive rocket spewing a column of flame during liftoff, and the periods of docking and solo flight by command and lunar modules also presented tense opportunities for problems to arise. The long gliding flight to and from the moon, however, was generally considered the least dangerous part of the trip, if indeed any portion of spaceflight can be considered safe or routine.

Because the lunar module was still attached and able to supply ample amounts of oxygen, electricity, and water, the crew at least had a means of sustaining themselves. And while the LM's engine had nowhere near the capacity of the engine in the command module, it did appear to have enough power to maneuver them onto the path that led back home.

Shortly after the accident, astronauts on the ground entered command and lunar module simulators and set to work in carefully constructed approximations of the conditions the *Apollo 13* crew was experiencing in their crippled spacecraft. Working around the clock, teams of flight controllers, engineers, and support staff throughout the space agency threw their collective will behind the effort to bring the crew safely back to earth.

Although they had survived the initial shock of the accident that had robbed them of the chance of completing a lunar landing, the crew of

Apollo 13 still faced several crucial challenges during their long flight. About five hours after the accident, still heading toward the moon, they had to fire the LM's engine to push the command-service-lunar module assembly back onto the "free-return trajectory"—the path that would carry them around the moon and, thanks to the moon's gravity, place them on a course leading directly back to earth.

Aquarius performed well during that first firing of its engines, much to the relief of the crew and everyone in mission control. The astronauts passed around the lunar far side without further difficulty. It was the second time in a little more than two years that Lovell had been that close to the surface of the moon without being able to touch down. This time, of course, the distractions were significant enough to numb any regret he may have felt about not landing.

Improvising an Air Filter

Despite all the careful calculations by the crew and by mission control, the want of a relatively simple air filter became a major, life-threatening concern.

In the closed environment of the *Apollo* spacecraft, the carbon dioxide that is the natural waste portion of human breath was trapped in the spacecraft's environmental control system (ECS) by a canister containing lithium hydroxide. Filtering the carbon dioxide was vital; at high levels it would cause illness and eventually death.

With the command module shut down, the crew had to rely on the lunar module's ECS, which consisted of two lithium hydroxide canisters that were together capable of filtering the carbon dioxide that two people would exhale during a period of about sixty hours. There were now three astronauts in the LM, of course, and they planned on a stay of more than four days. The problem was obvious, but the solution—replace the canisters in the LM with extras from the command and service module—was not. The LM filters were round; the proposed replacements were square.

The canisters onboard were allowed to operate past their estimated sixty-hour limit and worked surprisingly well for a total of 107 hours, although levels of carbon dioxide did rise well above the desired limit. The crew also had a single spare round canister that was rated for about forty hours, which they held on to as a last resort while the problem was worked on back in Houston.

Using only materials that they knew the astronauts had aboard the spacecraft, mission control staffers worked out an improvised retrofit for the square canisters. They hurriedly radioed the quick fix to the crew, who followed the directions carefully and pieced together the new filters. Carbon dioxide levels within the LM fell precipitously, and the astronauts were, at least for the time being, safe again.[13]

Having put the moon behind them, the crew was faced with the need to fire the LM's engine again, to put them on a faster path back to earth so they could return before their dwindling supplies of electricity and water ran out. With no air to move it away, the debris cloud from the accident had stubbornly clung to the side of the spacecraft, cutting the astronauts' view of the stars and thereby limiting their ability to position themselves accurately for the course adjustment.

Taking a page from ancient seaborne navigators, Lovell suggested that they use the sun for guidance, as it was the only star free of reflection from all the junk floating around them. Mission control agreed, and the engine burn went off without a hitch, bringing *Apollo 13* and its three cold, tired occupants a bit closer to home.[14]

Viewing the Damage

As they neared earth, the time came to jettison the service module—the location of the still-mysterious accident that had caused all the trouble. It was a simple procedure, performed on every flight, but in this case the astronauts were particularly interested in viewing the service module after letting it go. And when they did, the magnitude of their ordeal became jarringly evident. One entire side of the service module was missing, with only a scarred hole where one of the two oxygen tanks had sat. The crew frantically snapped photos of the damage, in the hope that they might be of use in determining the cause of the accident during the inevitable postflight investigation.

When they moved into the final hours of the ordeal, mission control radioed a detailed procedure—largely worked out by their fellow astronauts in the ground-based simulators—for bringing the dormant command module back to life.

The batteries that provided electricity to the command module were normally charged by the service module's fuel cells, which had been lost to the accident. So in order to get *Odyssey* up and running again, the crews on the ground had to find a way to feed it a charge from the lunar module's batteries. Luck was once again on the side of the *Apollo 13*'s crew; although there was no electrical channel that ran from the command and service modules to the lunar module when the spacecraft left the ground, there was a sensor circuit that the astronauts plugged in after the craft were linked in space. Although it was intended as a means of monitoring the lunar module's energy use, its path was reversed in this case, allowing current to slowly drain from the LM into the command module's batteries, providing enough power to revive *Odyssey* for the reentry trip.[15]

The command module displayed remarkable resiliency as it nodded back to life, and the crew moved back into the reborn craft, transferring from the lunar module that had sustained them for four cold, dark days. Lovell's last task before leaving the LM was to manually orient the craft so that whatever remained of its burning wreckage after reentry would fall into the Atlantic Ocean. For a few moments, the *Apollo 13* commander maneuvered the steering mechanism of the lunar module that he was to have guided to the lunar surface. On the way out of the moonship for the final time, he gathered up some souvenirs of the journey that was not to be. He would return to earth with the helmet he would have worn in the moon's Fra Mauro Highlands, and the plaque intended to enshrine the names of the *Apollo 13* crew on the lunar surface.[16]

Once the crew was back in *Odyssey*, the hatch was closed and the lunar module was jettisoned. "Farewell, *Aquarius*, and we thank you," said astronaut capcom Joe Kerwin in Houston as Lovell, Haise and Swigert watched the LM slowly drift away.

Finally, on April 17, 1970, *Apollo 13* returned safely to earth, splashing down just four miles away from the prime recovery ship, the USS *Iwo Jima*.

The crew was alive, suffering surely from the effects of their ordeal, dehydrated (the downside of their remarkable efficiency at conserving water), haggard, fatigued, and thinner (Lovell lost fourteen pounds during the trip) but alive.

Haise was particularly ill, with a fever of 103 degrees and an infection that took weeks to clear. But all three astronauts had survived without lasting detriments to their health.[17]

The Investigation

NASA administrator Thomas Paine, who would leave the agency's top post five months later, ordered an inquiry into the Apollo accident just hours after the crew's successful splashdown in the Pacific. The commission investigating the near-tragedy was chaired by Edgar Cortright, director of NASA's Langley Research Center in Virginia, and included Neil Armstrong among its members. Within two months, the Cortright Commission issued its report.

The origins of the incident that derailed *Apollo 13* apparently stretched as far back as 1965, when, according to the report, the power supplies for Apollo spacecraft were changed from twenty-eight to sixty-five volts, but the manufacturer of the craft's oxygen tanks failed to accommodate the change. As a result, the potentially dangerous tanks had flown on every Apollo mission up to and including *Apollo 13*.

A telling difference with the particular tank that wrecked the service module on *Apollo 13* was that it had been slightly damaged prior to the *Apollo 10* mission, on which it was scheduled to fly. It was repaired and installed in *Apollo 13*, and even though crews continued to have problems with the tank prior to the launch, it was deemed acceptable; thus the seeds of the accident were sown.[18]

8

Before the Short Day Ends:
Apollo in Twilight

After the near-miss of *Apollo 13*, fourteen months passed before the next flight lifted off. In the interim, two more missions were cut from the project; *Apollo 17* would be the last of the series.[1]

As the agency prepared for the next launch, in January 1971, the stakes were high—for the program, for future missions, and for the mission commander, Alan Shepard. He had finally returned to active flight status, his debilitating inner-ear condition cured by surgery, and he was commanding a mission aimed at landing on the moon. Accompanying him were command pilot Stuart Roosa and lunar module pilot Edgar Mitchell.

Apollo 14: Exploring the Moon

Equipped with an extra oxygen tank and spare battery, and buoyed by more than $10 million worth of technical modifications that had been recommended by the Cortright Commission following its investigation of the *Apollo 13* accident, *Apollo 14* lifted off on January 31, 1971. A problem cropped up early: when Roosa turned the *Kitty Hawk* command module around and attempted to dock with the lunar module, which the crew had dubbed *Antares*, the two craft refused to snap together.[2]

Responding as they had when *Apollo 13* had experienced its difficulties, crews on the ground immediately attempted to simulate the docking, but not knowing what the problem was, they were initially unable to create any problems for the simulations to solve. While they were successfully docking, *Apollo 14* was not, and time and fuel were running short.

After several more tries, a possible solution was radioed up from mission control. On the off chance that the command module probe had somehow not been sufficiently cleaned, there could be some small debris that was interfering with its connection to the lunar module. The plan, then, was to discard all elements of finesse and simply ram the probe into the LM's drogue receptacle, jarring loose any interfering debris in the process.

The crew took a deep breath, Roosa fired up *Kitty Hawk* and lunged it toward *Antares*, which was still stuck in the third stage of the Saturn V, and the two craft slammed together. The connection was solid. *Apollo 14* continued on toward the moon, its chance for a landing still intact.[3]

While Roosa worked on the linking problem, lunar module pilot Mitchell conducted an experiment in extrasensory perception that would later cause a minor controversy. The experiment, in which he envisioned a series of numbers in a particular order while several people back on earth tried to guess the order, was not authorized by NASA. Although it was a harmless and perhaps beneficial test of the effects of the space environment on telepathy and ESP, the fact that it had not been approved by the space agency prior to the flight caused the press to judge it harshly afterward. The results were interesting but inconclusive: two of the four subjects who tried to guess the number sequence scored better than random chance would dictate.[4]

With the docking problem solved, the trip to the moon proceeded as planned, but another problem cropped up just as Shepard and Mitchell were about to land. A short circuit in the lunar module's abort switch nearly triggered the abort program in the craft's onboard computer, just short of the instant at which the fast-descending spacecraft would make its final preparations for landing.

The astronauts found that they could dim the offending warning light by banging on the LM's instrument panel, and mission control quickly isolated a faulty switch as the source of the problem. The NASA team controlling the flight assembled its far-flung hardware and software experts from the Massachusetts Institute of Technology and Grumman's aerospace division, and a crash reprogramming of the LM software was begun. Consisting of sixty new pieces of code that had to be relayed to the crew and then flawlessly entered by Mitchell into the LM's computer, the new program waved off the automatic abort sequence but also deactivated a portion of the craft's computer guidance system. The change in plans translated into a near-total reliance on the abilities of the crew: due to the time constraints, Mitchell had to reprogram the computer accurately and immediately, and without the automatic abort sequence, Shepard's manual control of the descent to the surface would have to be nearly perfect.[5]

Fortunately for everyone involved, Mitchell's keyboarding was superb, and Shepard flawlessly piloted the lunar module down onto the Fra Mauro Highlands, the geologically rich spot that had originally been selected as the landing site for *Apollo 13*. They set down on a slight incline of about eight degrees, which gave their home on the moon an awkward tilt that made it more difficult to move around and much harder to sleep. The awkward lean did not interfere with the landing or the later ascent from the surface, however, so it had no serious overall impact on the mission.[6]

As they prepared for the first of their two planned extravehicular activities (EVAs), Shepard told Houston they were getting ready "to go out and play in the snow." The goals of the first walk were similar to those of earlier flights; thus the two astronauts set up the television camera, raised the American flag, and retrieved the package of experiments from the side of the lunar module.[7]

They presented an eerie spectacle when they set off into the distance to deploy the experiments. Because of the rolling, undulating terrain, they occasionally dropped out of view as they hit a low point in the landscape. The illusion that they were disappearing into the troughs was unsettling, even as they remained in radio contact and immediately re-emerged at the next high point.[8]

They trailed a wire-framed handcart that made it easier to collect rocks and surface samples. The cart, which NASA referred to as the modular equipment transporter (MET), seemed decidedly low-tech in comparison with the spacecraft and the astronauts themselves, resplendent in their bulky spacesuits, but it certainly made the job of retrieving samples easier and more productive. With it, Shepard and Mitchell were able to gather ninety-five pounds of lunar rocks.[9]

The astronauts returned to *Antares* for a few fitful hours of sleep. The task was even more difficult than on previous missions because of the lunar module's odd lean; both Shepard and Mitchell had to occasionally fight off the thought that the LM might tip over.[10]

They were appreciative when Houston agreed to cut the scheduled rest period short, and anxious to begin their second EVA. It turned out to be one of the most arduous of all the moon walks.

A Long, Hard Climb

After a brief stop to collect some samples, take photographs, and measure the moon's magnetic field with a portable magnetometer, Shepard and Mitchell set off for Cone Crater. Targeted by geologists who longed to test samples from it, the crater was believed to be a prime source of material that had been displaced when the Mare Imbrium basin was formed. Samples from Cone Crater would be extremely valuable to scientists trying to piece together the puzzle of the moon's origin and development.

For the astronauts, however, the crater presented a formidable task. It was a fair way off to begin with, and once at its base, they were faced with a relatively steep climb in their bulky pressure suits. The handcart may also have slowed their progress a bit, but in any case the climb would not have been easy. Finally, it wasn't entirely necessary; although part of the objective was to see whether or not they could make it to the crater's rim, to test the ability of astronauts to maneuver on the lunar surface, the samples they could find at any distance along the slope would still be of immense interest to the scientists back on earth.

They made two stops to rest before the word came from Houston that they need go no further. Shepard seemed to agree with mission control, but Mitchell favored continuing the climb. When capcom Fred Haise mildly argued the point, Mitchell replied, "I think you're finks."

Haise and Shepard relented a bit, and the climb went on. Eventually they had to stop before reaching the rim, but they still managed to collect a bunch of interesting samples, and the trip down the slope proved much easier.[11]

Despite the physical exertion it took, the long walk and difficult climb made it clear that astronauts could travel a healthy distance across the lunar landscape without undue fears about their ability to get back to the lunar module.

Shepard also had an experiment of his own to perform. Playing to the camera, he attached the head of a golf club, a six iron, to the long handle of the contingency sample collector, and then pulled a golf ball from a pocket in his spacesuit. Dropping the ball onto the rocky ground, he swung the awkward club with one hand and sent the tiny white sphere skipping along the surface. A second shot flew upward, sailing away only slightly hindered by the weak pull of lunar gravity, Shepard following it out of sight with an endearing play-by-play: "There it goes! Miles and miles and miles!"[12]

Their work and play completed, Shepard and Mitchell returned to *Antares*, reunited with Roosa in *Kitty Hawk*, and safely splashed down on February 9, 1971.

In April, James C. Fletcher took over as NASA administrator. He would oversee the agency for much of the 1970s, throughout the remaining moon landings, the *Skylab* missions, and the Apollo-Soyuz Test Project.

The Soviets Change Plans

Following the first American moon landing, the Soviet Union literally lowered its sights, concentrating more on long-duration earth orbit flights and the construction of an orbiting space station than on continued efforts to get to the moon. The Soviets did continue to develop the necessary spacecraft for a lunar mission, and according to information released in 1991, they attempted an unmanned lunar-related launch as late as November 23, 1972, with unhappy results, as the assembly's N-1 booster blew up about two minutes into the flight. In light of the four massive failures of the booster whose fiery temperament had definitively cost the Soviets their chance to beat the Americans to the moon, *future* development of the N-1 rocket was canceled in May 1974. The last Zond spacecraft was *Zond 8*, launched on October 20, 1970. Unmanned, it orbited the moon successfully and splashed down in the Indian Ocean.

Although they never landed a cosmonaut on the moon, the Soviets did land several sample-return craft similar to the one that crashed onto the surface during the *Apollo 11* flight. The first successful sampler was *Luna 16*, in September 1970, and *Luna 17* deployed *Lunokhod 1*, a small remote-controlled rover, two months later. Guided from earth, the tiny craft roamed the lunar surface for months before it stopped operating. The Soviets continued to send sample-return flights to the moon for several more years; the last was *Luna 24*, in August 1976.[13]

As the manned moon program declined, the totalitarian Soviet regime attempted to rewrite the history of the Russian space program, eliminating all evidence that the USSR had ever been trying to mount a manned launch. The lie dovetailed nicely with the program's new goal of developing a habitable earth satellite, as though that had been the aim all along, and the fiction gained some credence over the years.

As is so often the case, however, the attempt to misrepresent one portion of history cost in credibility elsewhere, and the government's ability to document any of its space exploits became suspect. Even the spectacular early achievements of the Soviet space program seemed tarnished as a result of the misinformation campaign. The truth about the program's successes and failures in space remained obscured until the Communist government fell from power two decades later.[14]

The facts that were evident at the time revealed the Russian program to be continuing on a course that was eerie in its parallels to the American Apollo project. Just as the sad death of cosmonaut Vladimir Komarov on *Soyuz 1* in April 1967 had followed shortly after the devastating *Apollo 1* fire, the Soviets experienced another space-related disaster during the year following the *Apollo 13* scare.

In June 1971, just fourteen months after *Apollo 13* safely returned to earth, *Soyuz 11* prepared for launch. The flight was to have been commanded by Alexei Leonov, who had so long ago taken the first spacewalk in history. A week before the launch, however, one of his fellow crew members was diagnosed with a lung ailment, and as a precautionary measure all three of the original cosmonauts were struck from the mission and replaced by the backup crew.

The mission launched on June 6, docked with the *Salyut* space station that had launched two months earlier, and the new crew of commander Georgi Dobrovolski, flight engineer Vladislav Volkov, and research engineer Viktor Patsayev accomplished its primary objective, setting a new record for long-endurance spaceflight.

During their return to earth, a valve intended to allow fresh air into the cabin to equalize its pressure after reentry became stuck open while the craft was still in space. The tiny breach of the capsule designed to protect them from the vacuum of space allowed their life-sustaining oxygen to escape within about a minute; fifteen seconds later the cosmonauts succumbed. They were found dead in their seats upon their return to earth. They had been in space for twenty-four days.[15]

Apollo 15: Toward a Better Understanding

Although public interest waned after the initial landing, the Apollo project grew in complexity and scientific value during the three years following the heroics of Armstrong, Aldrin, and Collins on *Apollo 11*. The last three voyages to the moon were particularly daring in scope and abundantly productive, thanks in large part to the additions of the lunar roving vehicle (LRV), or "rover," as it became affectionately known—an electric moon car that enabled the astronauts to cover a much wider area of the surface—and the addition of longer and more ambitious EVAs, which NASA labeled "traverses" to differentiate them from the brief excursions of past missions.[16]

The first of the last three Apollo missions was *Apollo 15*, commanded by Dave Scott. His previous flights had been the *Apollo 9* first workout of the lunar module and the harrowing *Gemini 8* spin with Neil Armstrong. James Irwin and Alfred Worden were along for the ride this time, Worden piloting the *Endeavor* command module and Irwin accompanying Scott to the lunar surface in the *Falcon* LM.

They blasted off on July 26, 1971, headed for the Hadley Rille valley, adjacent to the moon's Apennine Mountains. The landing site was mainly selected for the rich geological samples it was expected to yield.

Touchdown on the lunar surface followed on July 30. Scott's reaction to his first step was thoughtful and deliberate; he said, "As I stand out here in the wonders of the unknown at Hadley, I realize a fundamental truth about our nature. Man must explore. And this is exploration at its greatest."[17]

Irwin joined him on the surface, and the two astronauts retrieved the rover from its storage bay on the side of the LM. The lunar hot rod had weathered the long trip in fairly good condition, except for the loss of its front-wheel steering. The back wheels were also capable of maneuvering, however, so the loss was negligible.

The rover's camera would prove an invaluable addition to the last three lunar expeditions. It provided better images, in color, and allowed ground controllers to view the activities of both astronauts at the same time—a great advantage during long-distance EVAs when scientists on the ground could direct the lunar walkers toward samples and sites that seemed interesting. And at the end of the mission, the electronic eye mounted on the "moon car" would also make it possible to watch the ascent stage of the LM blast off.

Most important, though, was that the rover allowed the astronauts to travel much farther from their LM base. On their first trip, as mission control enjoyed its undulating view of the lunar surface passing beneath their wheels at the speed of about seven miles per hour, Scott and Irwin visited the base of the Apennines and scanned the long, low Hadley Rille valley.

They also set up another instruments package, which, given their landing location, was a particularly important task. Operating in conjunction with the instruments left behind by earlier missions, the new package now allowed the triangulation necessary for NASA to precisely locate future lunar events such as meteoroid crashes or earthquakes.

The instrument deployment also provided a moment of comic relief. As part of someone's idea of an experiment, Scott was supposed to toss the packaging from the instruments as far as possible. In his awkward spacesuit and trying to balance himself in the weak lunar gravity, the athletic Apollo commander gave the debris a wheezy heave that approximated the effort of a first-time discus thrower, tipping to one side and then wheeling completely out of sight of the camera. He was unhurt, and joked about the incident with mission control before closing out the EVA and returning to the lunar module.[18]

The Genesis Rock

During their next visit to the surface, the astronauts were surprised to find the front-wheel drive of their rover miraculously restored. They drove off happily to their next scheduled stops, one of which would yield what many scientists later regarded as the most important single sample of the entire Apollo program.

The chunk of lunar crust they dug up during that second EVA has since been dubbed the "Genesis rock" for all the clues it has provided scientists attempting to determine how the moon and earth were formed. Undisturbed by the impact of objects from space or the internal rumbling of moonquakes for millions of years, the sample that Scott and Irwin dug out of the surface of the moon had been formed during the earliest history of the solar system. It was an extraordinary find, and a concrete example of the value of the manned landing program.

Pushing hard on the special drill NASA engineers had created for the job, Scott's initial efforts to extract lunar core samples were harsh exercises in frustration. He would have bruises on his hands for several weeks after the mission, but all the hard work paid off in the long run, as he managed to fish out the deepest sample of all the Apollo missions. The eight-and-a-half-foot core sample of lunar dirt that *Apollo 15* brought back to earth revealed a great deal about the composition of the crust that lay beneath the lunar surface.[19]

After their second rest period, the astronauts completed their moon expedition with a ride to Hadley Rille and a walk a short way into the gaping valley, where they collected several more samples. Then, having accomplished their "hard science" objectives, the astronauts turned their efforts to more relaxed activities.

Proud to "have the opportunity to play postman," Scott hand-canceled a U.S. postage stamp—the first of several that the astronauts later passed on to a third party for private sale as unique collectibles. This unfortunately resulted in a controversy about the astronauts' profiting from their mission that echoed the criticism leveled at the *Mercury 7* astronauts when they agreed to sell the story of their exploits to *Life* magazine years earlier.[20]

After canceling the stamp, Scott then made a hands-on demonstration of Galileo's theory of gravity. Holding a hammer in one hand and a feather (appropriately enough, from a falcon, in honor of the LM) in the other, Scott invoked Galileo as one of the great minds whose contributions to science had helped bring humanity to the moon. He then dropped the hammer and the feather simultaneously, allowing them to drift through the nearly nonexistent lunar gravity. As Galileo had predicted, they hit the ground at the same time.[21]

According to plan, Scott and Irwin performed unprecedented chores on the moon, traveling farther and staying longer than their fellow astronauts had on previous missions. At the same time, floating overhead in lunar orbit in *Endeavor*, Al Worden's responsibilities as command module pilot were also expanded compared to those of his predecessors. A special camera and experiment bay, dubbed the scientific instrument module (SIM), had been added to the service module stage of the Apollo. The command module pilot was charged with operating the SIM devices in lunar orbit, and also would retrieve the film later in the mission. The necessity of a nonlunar EVA invoked memories of the program's past; when Worden left the *Apollo 15* craft a few days later, some 172,000 miles above the earth, he was the first person to walk in space since Buzz Aldrin had floated out of *Gemini 12*, back in 1966.[22]

Apollo 15 was a remarkable success. In addition to all it accomplished on the surface and Worden's considerable achievements aloft, it also launched a tiny satellite into lunar orbit—the first satellite ever released from a manned spacecraft—and during its study of black hole phenomena, it provided a rare opportunity for cooperation between the United States and the USSR, when an earth-based Russian observatory examined the same spots the Apollo craft was observing at the same time, so the data from each could be correlated.

Some 1,400 photographs and 169 pounds of lunar rocks were also counted on the good side of the ledger when Scott, Irwin, and Worden splashed down on August 4. A scary moment preceded their return when one of their three main parachutes failed to open. Fortunately, two chutes were plenty to slow their descent, and they splashed down safely.[23]

Scott was philosophical at the postflight press conference. He recalled the special plaque the crew had left on the surface, commemorating the fourteen astronauts and cosmonauts who had died during the twinned American and Soviet space programs. Alongside the plaque, a heart-wrenching memento recalled the sacrifices it invoked, in the form of a tiny figure lying face down in the lunar dust, symbolically representing the fallen space explorers.

Quoting Plutarch, the Apollo commander tried to put the mission, and the grand adventure of lunar exploration, in proper perspective. "The mind is not a vessel to be filled," he said with a gentle smile, "but a fire to be lighted."[24]

Apollo 16: Twenty Hours on the Moon

Long-time veteran John Young was selected to command *Apollo 16*, sharing the mission with Ken Mattingly and Charlie Duke, who had been on the primary and backup crews of *Apollo 13*. Duke's exposure to German measles had caused the flight surgeons to bump Mattingly off the nearly disastrous flight; now they would go into space together.

Another precarious preflight dilemma cropped up when staffers at the Marshall Space Flight Center had difficulty determining the cause of a problem with the launch vehicle's gyroscope two days before the scheduled launch. They finally gave the flight their approval to proceed less than an hour before liftoff, on April 16, 1972.

While nothing else extraordinary popped up during the first part of the journey, another, potentially more serious oddity arose just after Young and Duke had floated off in the *Orion* lunar module. Alone in the amusingly named *Casper* command module, Mattingly was suddenly faced with a fault in the spaceship's backup control system. Although the main system was still functioning properly, the loss of the backup system just prior to the moon landing made the entire mission much riskier. For safety's sake, *Casper* and *Orion* were brought back into close proximity while ground crews ran through simulations of the problem. After six hours of sorting through the potential dangers involved, the threat was determined to be less severe than originally thought, and a workaround was found.[25]

The landing was back on track, and Young and Duke were obviously elated at the prospect and the actual event, they were also exhausted from the long delay. Although they were scheduled to begin their lunar activities right away after they touched down in the Descartes Highlands, they slept first.

Once they were on the surface, Young set up an ultraviolet camera that provided scientists on earth their first astronomical observations from a moon-based instrument. Further experiments were also going well when the unwieldy pressure suits and strange low-gravity environment made its first serious impact on the astronauts' activities. Struggling with the long, meshy lines of the gear designed to test lunar heat flow, Young was tripped up and inadvertently pulled the entire assembly down. He wasn't hurt, but the experiment was put out of commission. Again earth-based crews simulated the damage and tried to come up with an acceptable repair procedure, but the limited amount of time the astronauts could spend on the surface forced them to simply forgo the experiment altogether. A replacement would be deployed on *Apollo 17* instead.[26]

Better news came from seismic experiments and a magnetometer measurement, during which Young recorded an unexpectedly intense magnetic field that surprised and delighted scientists when they studied the data later on. The Apollo commander also put the lunar rover to a bouncing, rollicking test, in preparation for the astronauts' later EVA tasks.

Their second trip out of *Orion* brought Young and Duke up the side of Stone Mountain, where they stopped at a crater and looked back at their lunar module, about four miles away and seven hundred feet below their new perch.

Their third EVA brought them north of the LM, to the largest crater that any Apollo crew would visit. They took rock samples and photographs, and looked over the edge of the deep crater.

And then they discovered a particularly interesting sample. The distance from the rover was hard to judge, but sitting somewhere relatively close by was what appeared to be a massive boulder. Unlike the small rock samples that they and the previous astronauts had come across, this rock seemed to loom taller and wider than both Young and Duke put together. They were fascinated by the huge, stony edifice, and set off for a closer look.[27] As they moved away from the camera, seemingly oblivious to mission control and entirely taken with the "house-sized rock," as it would later come to be known, someone in Houston joked in mock narration, "As our crew slowly disappears into the sunset . . . "[28]

As it turned out, the house-sized rock was within easy walking distance, and the astronauts had no difficulty returning to the rover after they had finished their close inspection. They returned to the LM, finished their moon chores, and lifted off and rendezvoused with Mattingly without incident. During their three trips outside the LM, they had spent more than twenty hours roaming the surface of the moon, and collected 208 pounds of lunar samples. For his part, command module pilot Mattingly successfully retrieved the SIM film canisters during his spacewalk, and *Apollo 16* splashed down, another resounding success, on April 27.[29]

Apollo 17: Lunar Science Advances

The last Apollo moon expedition would be the longest of the series, lasting more than twelve days, and it was the only Apollo to launch after dark. Gene Cernan, the *Gemini 9* and *Apollo 10* veteran, was the mission's commander, and Ronald Evans—whose prior flying experience included more than a hundred combat missions in Vietnam—piloted the command module, *America*. And for this last Apollo on the moon, a professional scientist would be along: Dr. Harrison "Jack" Schmitt, a geologist, would see up close and in their natural setting the lunar samples that his fellow scientists could examine only in the sterile confines of earth laboratories.

America was the name the crew chose for its command module, and for all those who had labored in the space program over the years, it was both appropriate and exquisitely poignant to hear the poetry of the word, charged with the symbolic weight of all the great expeditions of the past, at each crucial juncture of the trip.

The launch on the night of December 7, 1972 quickly took Cernan, Schmitt, and Evans into earth orbit; they began circling the moon three days later. For Cernan and Schmitt, the target was the Taurus-Littrow region of the lunar landscape, among the moon's more recently formed areas, at least in terms of the cosmic clocks that measure evolution in ages rather than time spans more familiar to human beings.

Following the landing, as he left the LM *Challenger*, Cernan stopped a moment for reflection, dedicating "the first step of Apollo Seventeen to all those who made it possible." There was a respectful sadness to the flag raising, as everyone associated with the space effort absorbed the melancholy image of the final Apollo moon crew saluting the nation that had birthed the long day of America's moon journey, and which now hastened it to safety as night began to fall.[30]

During the first EVA there were more core samples, and the heat flow experiment went up much more easily this time. The astronauts sang together as they worked, the time passed easily, and the only real difficulty they encountered was the cloud of dust that the lunar rover occasionally kicked up, the result of a broken rear fender they'd sustained during their travels. Even on the moon, it seemed, there were fender-bending ruts and rocks to be overcome.

Fresh from his own rover experiences on *Apollo 16*, John Young pitched in his effort on the ground, helping to concoct a fix that involved a stiff lunar map, some tape, and some spare clamps. Cernan and Schmitt put the plan into action during their next excursion, and it worked entirely as advertised. They had no further trouble with the fender for the rest of their stay.[31]

A Colorful Discovery

During that second EVA they took more samples, and at one point kicked around a boulder that looked about the size of a basketball. The big surprise of the day, however—indeed, the surprise of the entire trip—occurred when the astronauts discovered orange soil. Scientists on earth were ecstatic at the find, and flight staffers at mission control had to remind both the scientists and the astronauts that time constraints dictated that the crew move on to other duties.[32]

The third and final EVA took Cernan and Schmitt to a harsh slope as they completed their journey through the long valley they had set out to explore. When it was finished, Schmitt returned to the LM first, leaving Cernan to take the last lunar steps of the Apollo program. "I believe that history will record that America's challenge of today has forged man's destiny of tomorrow," Cernan said, commemorating the moment.[33]

The plaque left on the lunar module descent stage reads, "Here man completed his first exploration of the Moon, December 1972 A.D. May the spirit of peace in which we came be reflected in the lives of all mankind."

The Apollo project placed twelve Americans on the surface of the moon, gathered 838 pounds of lunar rock samples and more than 30,000 high-resolution photographs, and involved more than 400,000 people in a peaceful enterprise designed to gather knowledge about the nature of human existence. The astronauts and their accomplishments inspired the nation at a particularly difficult time, as America weathered the transition from the relative peace and prosperity of the late 1950s to the searching, angry dissent of the 1960s, fueled by the deepening war in Vietnam and civil unrest and violence at home.[34]

In their lunar visits, bearing the peaceful intent of all humanity, the astronauts were the embodiment of the ideals of courage and hope. On the desolate moon, in their awkward landing craft with its spindly legs and thin walls, their fragile presence bespoke the nature of their mission: to simply be there amid that ancient dust. They expanded the view of their fellow humans while at the same time trying to relate some measure of the enormousness of their personal experience. With open minds and eager hearts, they brought peace as their gift to the heavens, and brought a positive joy to those who followed them from the earth.

9

Skylab: A Place in Space

Although the long-term vision of those caught up in the romance of America's moon journeys saw a permanent lunar presence somewhere in the nation's future, the cost and complexity involved in that type of commitment probably excluded it from the first phase of space exploration from the very beginning, even if such tantalizing historical what-ifs as the Kennedy assassination and the long slide into Vietnam were reversed.

But if the prospect of lunar real estate was out of the question, NASA still entertained serious hopes of securing at least a semicontinuous presence in space, preferably close enough to the earth to allow the still-developing space shuttle to eventually drop in for a visit.

Thus the agency hatched *Skylab*, America's answer to the Soviets' *Salyut* space station. Using hardware left over from the three scuttled lunar missions that had been cut from the Apollo program, the *Skylab* plan called for the launch of a Saturn V whose third stage could be used as an orbiting home and work area for successive crews of astronauts, who would remain in the structure for stays of one to two months at a time. The crews could be sent via less powerful rockets, in leftover capsules that would have served as the command modules of the final moonbound Apollos.

The technology reuse promised to keep the program's cost down (in relative terms, compared to the cost of the lunar missions); operating the station in earth orbit would be less complex and therefore—or so the argument went—safer than the long journey to the moon; and finally, the continuity would keep NASA's highly prized collection of experienced aerospace engineers together and their expertise up to date in the years leading to the space shuttle era.[1]

Skylab 1: Hardware Problems

Skylab was launched on May 14, 1973. A problem became evident shortly after the lab reached its orbit 270 miles from earth, when it became obvious to mission control that the facility's meteor shield had broken off, exposing the lab's workshop area to the searing heat of the sun, which would make it uninhabitable. As it went, the shield also ripped away one of the two solar panels that supplied *Skylab*'s electrical power; and the second panel was jammed with debris from the shield, which prevented it from deploying properly.[2]

Skylab 2: The Crew Catches Up

After eleven days of frantic simulation and testing, the first *Skylab* crew set off to fix the ailing station, lifting off on May 25. *Apollo 12* commander Pete Conrad helmed the first *Skylab* crew, adding the mission to a resume that would hence forth always begin with "walked on the surface of the moon." Traveling with him to the damaged space station were Paul Weitz and Joe Kerwin, who had the added distinction of being the first American physician in space.

They fitted the crippled lab with a tarplike "parasol" that had been hurriedly improvised to replace the destroyed meteor shield and lower the temperature of *Skylab*'s orbital workshop. The parasol turned out to be a pretty good solution, although the astronauts still had to struggle with the remaining solar panel later in the trip. Once they pulled the panel free of its obstructions and popped it into place, the station began to soak up energy from the sun according to plan, and the power available inside the floating lab doubled. The fix allowed the crew to conduct many of the experiments they had initially been assigned, and salvaged many of the mission's original objectives.

Conrad, Kerwin, and Weitz returned to earth on June 22, after twenty-

eight days in space. They had performed exceptionally well under trying circumstances, making the necessary repairs and carrying out a good
portion of the experiments planned for the trip.[3]

Skylab 3: Long Day's Work

Conrad's fellow *Apollo 12* moon explorer Alan Bean commanded the
second Skylab mission. They had been the third and fourth people to
walk on the moon, and their presence lent the fledgling space station a
good deal of luster—particularly important in view of the program's
difficult beginning. In addition to Bean, the *Skylab 3* crew (the lab itself
had been designated *Skylab 1*; Conrad's mission was *Skylab 2*) also featured Jack Lousma and scientist-astronaut Owen Garriott.

They faced a potential crisis early on, when it was discovered that
their command module was leaking fuel. Talk of a possible rescue mission proved premature, however, when the problem was determined to
be less serious than originally thought.

Freed of worries about their well-being during their ride home, the
crew settled down to work, frequently stretching their day at the orbiting
office to a length of twelve hours or so. Their torrid pace allowed them
to complete all the experiments they had originally been assigned and
some unexpected additional tests before the fifty-nine-day mission came
to an end on September 25.[4]

Skylab 4: Science Gains

The final *Skylab* crew launched on November 16, 1973. Gerald Carr
was the commander, accompanied by William Pogue and scientist-
astronaut Ed Gibson. None of the astronauts had flown in space before,
and the harsh pace demanded of them by ground controllers presented a
serious challenge during the early part of the mission. Following the
course of their predecessors, however, they managed to turn the rough
start into an impressively successful mission.

Highlights included photographs of Comet Kohoutek, whose existence had just been discovered in January, and Gibson's start-to-finish
profile of a solar flare. The crew also completed EVAs that totaled more
than twenty-two hours, and they spent eighty-four days in space, the
long-duration record at the time.

When they returned to earth on February 8, 1974, the last *Skylab*

crew left the station in a slightly higher orbit than usual, hoping to pro-
long its useful life into the shuttle era, which was still years away even
in NASA's most optimistic estimations. The agency shut the lab down
after Carr, Pogue, and Gibson left, and the forlorn space station twirled
around the earth a blind, dormant cocoon for the next four years.[5]

Skylab's Fall to Earth

Revived from the ground in 1978, *Skylab*'s apparently imminent fall
from orbit caused a maelstrom of criticism to descend on the space agency.
Fears that pieces of the returning lab would survive reentry and rain
flaming wreckage down on heavily populated areas were exacerbated
by the fact that the plummet watch continued well into 1979.

NASA did its best to allay the public's fears, and to control the descent when it finally occurred, on July 12, 1979. Unfortunately, the agency
wasn't entirely successful at either task; the bad publicity did nothing to
help its image, and pieces of *Skylab* did survive reentry to impact the
earth, although only in relatively sparsely inhabited regions of Australia, where they resulted in no reported injuries or property damage.[6]

Its controversial demise denied *Skylab* much of the praise it rightfully
deserved for its scientific contributions and the valiant attempts of its
astronauts to further the cause of human space exploration. Data from
Skylab experiments helped to expand scientists' understanding of the
workings of the sun, the impact of long-duration missions on the human
body, and the effects of the vacuum of space on materials-processing
procedures. Had the lab been able to remain aloft into the 1980s, a shuttle
might have been able to pitch it into a higher orbit, prolonging its mission and lengthening its legacy.

In many ways, the space station was a very good idea at a particularly
poor time. Following the Apollo moon missions was as unenviable a
task as any space effort could be assigned, and the wait for the space
shuttle, for which the lab could have served as a celestial destination,
turned out to be too long.

Two decades after *Skylab* was shuttered, following previously unthinkable political realignments on earth, the Soviet space station *Mir*
would provide a place for American astronauts to work among the stars.
In its testament to the human spirit, that cooperation provided some
small tip of the hat to the Skylab ideal, and to the people who gave the
project life.

Despite the serious nature of their work and the fact that their careers as astronauts required them to risk their lives each time they entered a capsule for a flight, the Mercury Seven projected an almost boyish charm in NASA's publicity photos. Here they pose with a model of the Atlas booster and Mercury space capsule, demonstrating the relative size of the rocket and the tiny spacecraft, and their own relative discomfort with posing for awkwardly staged public relations collateral. Seated, left to right, are Gus Grissom, Scott Carpenter, Deke Slayton, and Gordon Cooper, while Alan Shepard, Wally Schirra, and John Glenn (l to r) look on. (*All photos from NASA unless otherwise credited.*)

Ed White, Gus Grissom, and Roger Chaffee (l to r), the crew of *Apollo 1*, were killed when their spacecraft caught fire during a test on January 27, 1967. The changes made to the Apollo spacecraft following their deaths were directly responsible for the safer passage of those who followed, and the loss of three men whose lives had been so intensely dedicated to the cause of space exploration forced NASA to rigorously reexamine every aspect of its program and procedures.

One of the single most enduring images from the space program's first era, this photo of the rising earth was taken by the *Apollo 8* astronauts as they completed their first turn around the moon after becoming the first human beings to ever enter lunar orbit. Celebrating Christmas Eve of 1968 orbiting the moon, the *Apollo 8* crew of Jim Lovell, Frank Borman, and Bill Anders took turns reading from the Book of Genesis, bringing the year to a close on a hopeful note for Americans weary of war, assassinations, violence, and political upheaval.

Dave Scott stands at the door of the command module *Gumdrop* during the flight of *Apollo 9*, in March 1969. Sharing the view with commander Jim McDivitt from the *Apollo 9* lunar module *Spider*, Rusty Schweickart recorded this image of Scott, who later landed on the moon as the commander of *Apollo 15*.

Neil Armstrong, Michael Collins, and Buzz Aldrin, the crew of *Apollo 11*. The first mission to place astronauts on the surface of the moon, *Apollo 11* inspired Americans at a pivotal time in U.S. history. While the nation weathered its transition from the relative peace and prosperity of the years following World War II to the tumultuous unrest of the 1960s, the Apollo project involved more than 400,000 people in a peaceful enterprise designed to gather knowledge about the nature of human existence. It placed twelve Americans on the surface of the moon, gathered 838 pounds of lunar rock samples and more than 30,000 high-resolution photographs, and in the quiet dedication of its engineers, administrators, academics, and astronauts, it embodied the ideals of human courage and hope.

Buzz Aldrin descends the steps of the lunar module as he prepares to walk on the moon. The astronauts who made the 240,000-mile trip to the lunar surface displayed an almost perfect professionalism in the face of grave risk, frequent physical discomfort, and the numbing stress of performing their epic tasks for an audience of hundreds of millions of their fellow human beings, literally watching their every move from the earth.

Footprints large and small mark humanity's first visit to the lunar surface as Buzz Aldrin stands near the footpad of the *Apollo 11* lunar module *Eagle* on July 20, 1969. Even though it was clear that humans landing on the moon would not likely face little green men, catastrophic changes in climate, or a terrain that would fall away beneath them, that first landing was still a feat as audacious as any ever undertaken before in human history

Apollo 11 lunar module pilot Buzz Aldrin deploys the Passive Seismic Experiment Package (PSE) on the moon's surface. When Aldrin and Neil Armstrong left the moon, the sensitive instrument was left behind to transmit data about meteorite impacts, lunar landslides, and moonquakes to scientists on earth. The scientific achievements of the Apollo program have broadened the scope and understanding of a wide array of academic disciplines, and have led to advances in engineering and product development methods that have transformed many once-futuristic designs into real-world commercial products.

No track in the lunar dust could adequately compensate those who lost a loved one in the effort to extend humanity's reach into the dominion of the stars, but none who were lost, in the program's early years or during the shuttle era, have been forgotten. This plaque, listing the names of those American astronauts and Soviet cosmonauts who died during the two superpowers' furious race into space, was left on the moon by Dave Scott and Jim Irwin on August 2, 1971. Undisturbed by wind or weather on the sterile surface of the moon for decades now, the little relic is also symbolic of the astronauts' capacity for understanding the expansive nature of their endeavors in terms that reflected the nation's commitment to the ideal that no technological advance, political advantage, or national space goal was worth more than a single human life.

The spindly-legged, sixteen-ton lunar module proved a resilient, if odd-looking, home to those astronauts who landed on the moon. Ironically, the lunar module's most important contribution came during the *Apollo 13* mission, when the crew was forced to crowd into the tiny, fragile craft for their long return trip to earth. Here, Buzz Aldrin works alongside the *Apollo 11* lunar module *Eagle*.

Curiosity about the moon — what it means, and why by some cosmic logic it has been placed "up there" to rise each dark night and then hide every glaring day — has caused human beings to think and to wonder throughout their history on earth. The twelve Apollo astronauts who landed on the lunar surface in the late 1960s and early 1970s have frequently expressed a similar awe in recalling those all too brief moments when they experienced the moon first-hand.

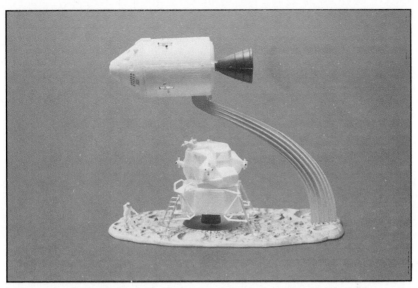

The American public's fascination with space travel launched countless products in the decades since the Mercury Seven first stepped into the national spotlight. Models like this vintage 1960s-era Apollo craft proved popular with youngsters who enjoyed the science of putting things together almost as much as they did the science of the space program. (*Photo courtesy Revell-Monogram, Inc.*)

The space program has given rise to a flood of toys, games, and collectibles ranging from the educational to those that are merely fun. This model of the lunar module, depicting astronauts working amid the barren moonscape, is part of a series of space-themed model kits that dates back to the earliest years of the space program. (*Photo courtesy Revell-Monogram, Inc.*)

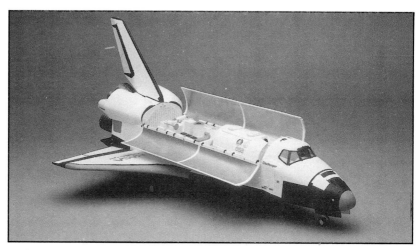

As the space program has made flying into the heavens seem almost prosaic in the shuttle era, with regular launches and a greatly increased number of individuals who have traveled in space, products depicting its progress have become more detailed and realistic. This model of the shuttle reveals the open bay of the complex craft as it looks in space. (*Photo courtesy Revell-Monogram, Inc.*)

Perhaps the most resounding echo of all that the space race and cold war eventually led to in international cooperation, the *Mir* space station played host to a number of U.S. astronauts in the 1990s. This model of the Russian space station, sold in toy stores throughout the United States, made the realities of the new era evident to a new generation of Americans in a most American fashion, adding the image of *Mir* to a long line of space-related icons that share a special place in the national consciousness. (*Photo courtesy Revell-Monogram, Inc.*)

10

Apollo-Soyuz Test Project: A Handshake Across the Heavens

Momentarily distracted by his uncharacteristically spry partner in space diplomacy, a bespectacled Leonid Brezhnev, president of the Soviet Union and chairman of the Presidium of the Supreme Soviet, looked over at U.S. president Richard Nixon like a grade-school child attempting to see his classmate's paper. Nixon motioned with his pen, passed some comment in an encouraging whisper, and then, having affixed his own signature to the document under consideration, smiled broadly and snapped shut the elegant blue binder containing his copy of the just-ratified agreement between the two space superpowers. A handshake, that most simple sign of human camaraderie, followed, giving birth to the hope that it would within three short years be echoed by the crews of U.S. and Soviet spacecraft high above the earth.[1]

A Unique Mission

The final flight of the Apollo program has receded in history as a sort of interesting anomaly, in retrospect of interest only to those associated with its development or otherwise interested in the history of the period. But it was part of a welcomed flush of friendship between the two great space powers, the United States and the Soviet Union, during a particularly difficult period, and a fitting end to the cycle of achievements that best demonstrated the exemplary national instincts that are the enduring Apollo legacy.

The last use of an Apollo craft in space was during the Apollo-Soyuz Test Project (ASTP) in July 1975. The mission, a joint project of NASA and the Soviet Academy of Sciences, was simple: for the first time, American and Russian citizens would join together in space via a rendezvous and docking of their separate vehicles, and the exchange of crew members from one craft to the other.

In both its technical and political considerations, the concept was revolutionary. The Soviet approach to space travel, different in many significant aspects from NASA's, had been known to the U.S. side throughout the 1960s only by way of surveillance provided by the U.S. intelligence community. For a joint mission to proceed, the technical differences—everything from the docking mechanism to the communications and guidance systems, the atmospheric conditions maintained in each craft, and crew transfer and flight control procedures—would have to be openly discussed, studied, and reconciled to ensure standardization.

Politically, the idea of a joint U.S.-Soviet space mission became much easier for the United States to pursue after the moon landing. The competition with the Soviets had long been a steely thread in the complex rationale for the long and dangerous space race; it often seemed unthinkable and even vaguely unpatriotic to envision a peaceful, multilateral international space venture until Americans had successfully visited the lunar surface at least once. After that goal had been achieved, and given the great store of goodwill and positive public reaction it generated, the way was clear for just about any new space-related initiative, and the seeds of ASTP were soon planted.

It was in that celebratory autumn of 1969, just weeks after the landing, that President Nixon gave his go-ahead to newly appointed NASA administrator Thomas Paine to initiate contacts with the Soviets, to determine the feasibility of a joint mission. The project went forward in earnest the following fall, when NASA administrators met with their Russian counterparts for the first time. Official sanction by both sides came in May of 1972, when Nixon and Brezhnev, during their first U.S.-

Soviet summit meeting, signed the agreement for a joint orbital mission that eventually became ASTP.[2]

Even with the mutual cooperation of the superpowers, the technical difficulties of the joint mission were daunting. The Soviets had long relied on the automatic control of their rendezvous and docking procedures from the ground, while the American approach granted a greater degree of autonomy to the astronauts piloting the spacecraft.

Philosophy aside, the necessary physical alterations to the docking mechanisms that had served each side long and well were extensive, to the degree that a completely new system was created by each.[3]

Further difficulties were caused by the "information drag" of the Soviet scientists' frequent delays in providing various technical data, due largely to the weight of the Soviet bureaucracy.[4]

Space Diplomacy

The program's eventual success is best attributed to the individuals involved. Scientists from the two vastly different cultures, laboring under enormous difficulties of technology, diplomacy, language, historical event, and received opinion, managed to surmount all barriers to their collective success and realize the envisaged mission less than five years from the moment of its first serious consideration.

In their conduct during their training and during the flight, American astronauts Tom Stafford, Donald "Deke" Slayton, and Vance Brand and Russian cosmonauts Alexei Leonov and Valeri Kubasov exemplified the project's good feelings and shared commitment. In addition to the usual rigors of preparing physically and mentally for a space mission, the crews had the additional task of learning each other's language—which, in the event, each group used throughout the training and the mission, the Americans speaking Russian and the Russians speaking English. It was a hard-won achievement for all, as the language training was difficult and extensive for all five crew members.[5]

Stafford, the commander of the Apollo craft, was the rendezvous expert among the group, with experience dating back to the first space rendezvous ever, on *Gemini 6* in 1965. He had practiced the procedure further as commander of *Gemini 9* the following year, and was part of the *Apollo 10* crew that had done the same with the lunar module in May 1969, just above the moon, a few months before the landing.

After backing up the *Apollo 15* and two *Skylab* crews, Vance Brand would fly into space for the first time as a member of the American ASTP team.

And Deke Slayton, so long ago sidelined from space by a heart condition and returned to flight status only in 1972, would also be making his first flight, at the age of fifty-one.

On the Soviet side, Alexeï Leonov had been the first human ever to walk in space, during the flight of *Voskhod 2* in 1965. Valeri Kubasov had been in space as a member of the *Soyuz 6* crew in 1969.

Even with the intensely individual emotions that each must have felt—Slayton, for example, finally getting his chance to fly in space after years of assigning others to take part in Apollo's most epic adventures—the five men well understood the symbolic importance of their effort. By all accounts, they got along famously, indulging each other personally as well as officially. The particulars changed depending on the geography: in America, the goodwill ambassadors enjoyed a celebratory visit to Disney World; in Russia, the overgrown rocket jockeys engaged in an old-fashioned snowball fight and broke out an impromptu Fourth of July celebration by unexpectedly setting off fireworks.[6]

The Soviets: Unprecedented Media Access

After years of planning and hard work, sometimes torturously slow exchanges of information, and difficult training of both crew and control teams, the mission was finally set to begin on July 15, 1975, with the launch of the Soviets' *Soyuz 19.*

The Baikonur Cosmodrome, the Soyuz launch facility, was located in the remote desert of what was in 1975 the Soviet Republic of Kazakhstan. The Soviets were the subject of some relatively restrained criticism by the Western press for not allowing foreign journalists to visit the Cosmodrome, but were also rightly praised for what was at the time a remarkable degree of openness for a Russian space flight.

The location of the Soviet facility was a particular sticking point for knowledgeable members of the American space hierarchy and intelligence community. Thanks to spy plane and satellite reconnaissance photos, U.S. officials had known for years that the Baikonur Cosmodrome was actually located several hundred miles southwest of the small mining town of Baikonyr, closer to the town of Tyuratam. As the Soviet space program grew over the years, Tyuratam had gradually vanished from all official maps, which merely showed empty desert where the town and the space facility were located.

Intelligence analysts waiting to see how—or if—the USSR would explain the discrepancies in its description of the space city's location soon had their answer when the Apollo crew was taken on a tour of the Cosmodrome. The astronauts were told that the facility was located in the city of "Leninsk."[7]

Despite the deception, the overall Soviet approach was more open than ever before. For the first time, the USSR released a press package to the Western news media prior to a space launch; the kit provided a flight plan for the Soyuz craft and an explanation of the experiments the cosmonauts were to undertake. And most significant, the *Soyuz 19* launch would be the first Soviet space shot ever broadcast live by Russian television, so even though foreign journalists would not be able to cover the event in person at the Baikonur Cosmodrome, they were free—from the confines of the press center set up for them at a Moscow hotel—to view the event as it happened, watching along with a large percentage of the rest of the world's citizenry.

For the Soviet Union, the access was unprecedented. Whatever its name, the city from which the launch would be made had been considered top secret for a long time, and in addition to its being rubbed off the map, its population of 50,000 had not been reported in the official census even as recently as 1970. Now, far beyond the initial hurdles of admitting its existence and admitting the area's importance to the nation's space effort, Soviet officials were permitting a live broadcast of the very activity they had so long sought to hide.

Leonov and Kubasov blasted off successfully from their Baikonur launch pad, climbing skyward out of the reportedly 104–degree heat of the Kazakhstan desert and shortly settling into an orbit around the earth with an apogee of 179 miles and perigee of 117 miles. The only glitch marring this first segment of the joint project was the failure of an onboard television camera, which the cosmonauts repaired during the following day, and then used to transmit live pictures back to earth.

Once mission control in Houston received confirmation from the Soviets that *Soyuz 19* had successfully attained its predetermined orbit, the Apollo crew of Stafford, Slayton, and Brand were given the go-ahead to launch. Their liftoff followed the Soviets' by seven and a half hours.[8]

The Americans: Apollo's Last Flight

Shortly into their flight, the Apollo crew extracted the docking module, following the same procedure as their moonbound brethren had in extracting their lunar modules, and then fired their positioning rockets to get into the proper orbital position for docking. A minor difficulty arose when a helium bubble developed in a propellant tank as they fired the rockets; it would have no effect on the mission.

At this point, the activities of the two separate crews began to take on a certain symmetry. As the cosmonauts labored to repair the onboard camera that was critical to recording any number of important events during the historic mission, including Apollo's approach as the two craft were to attempt their linkup, the astronauts discovered and repaired problems with several recalcitrant latches on the two-ton docking module. While they played Mr. Fix-It for the unexpected difficulties, both crews also continued to move into the new orbits necessary for their planned rendezvous and docking.

Finally, on July 17, the appointed moment arrived. Each crew could see the other's craft approach, the Americans floating forward in their bright silver cylinder, the Russians maneuvering ever closer in their long, bluish green tube.

In Apollo, the word came up from Houston: "Apollo, Houston. I've got two messages for you. Moscow is go for docking; Houston is go for docking. It's up to you guys. Have fun." And the response: "All right. It sounds good."

Once the two spacecraft were in position, directly facing each other, the Russians were able to make out the cylindrical "silver dollar" shape of the Apollo, its propulsive tail hidden behind the round outline of its shining body, with the blunt gray button of the docking module in its center.

The American view was of the near end of the elongated bluish green Soyuz bug, flat at the far side, with a circular collar reaching forward from the bulbous ball of the craft's near face. Apollo's camera captured the shudder of the docking as the two strange birds, suddenly more elegant than ever before by virtue of what their linking signified to those who watched from far below, clamped together, swaying and heaving at the point of impact, 140 miles above the earth.[9]

Command centers in both countries were a sea of smiles as scientists and engineers who had worked long and hard to give the project life took a moment to celebrate the triumph of their elegant technological achievement over the chaos of their momentarily suspended competition.

Formality and familiarity went hand in hand in defining the project's unique tone; when the two spacecraft met, the American commander Stafford could be heard confirming the link: "We have capture." In the spirit of the moment, the Soviet commander, Leonov, replied, "Well done, Tom."[10]

Stafford and Slayton moved into the docking module a short while later. Because the atmospheric conditions in the Apollo and Soyuz crafts were different, with the Soviets breathing a mixture of nitrogen and oxygen similar to that on earth, at a different pressure than the Americans, who breathed pure oxygen, the-ten-foot long docking module doubled as an airlock which allowed crew members to adapt gradually to the atmosphere of the craft they were about to enter.

Linked Flight and Crew Transfer

As soon as the astronauts were comfortably adapted to the conditions they would encounter upon entering *Soyuz 19*, the last of the barriers—technical, political, cultural, historical, and now physical—had fallen. Stafford met Leonov at the opened Soyuz hatch with a firm handshake and a single word: "*Tovarich*," the Russian word for "friend." Leonov's response, in English, was as typically American in its sentiment as in its words: "Very happy to see you. How are things?"

The three men then embraced and continued on into *Soyuz 19*. The crews exchanged flags and plaques commemorating the event, and Leonov presented the Apollo crew with a portrait he had drawn of them during their training exercises.[11]

For forty-seven hours the American Apollo and Soviet Soyuz circled the earth as a single entity. There were further crew exchanges, with each group sharing a meal in the other's compartment; further exchanges of gifts, including seeds to be planted in each other's country once the crews had returned to earth; and a joint televised news conference, during which Tom Stafford expressed the hope that the project had "opened a new era in the history of mankind." There were also messages of congratulations from Leonid Brezhnev and from U.S. president Gerald Ford, who spoke to the crew live at some length.[12]

On July 19 the two spacecraft undocked and flew separately but close by each other for a little more than three hours. During their flight apart they performed several joint experiments, including one where Apollo created an artificial solar eclipse, during which Kubasov photographed the outer reaches of the sun's corona.

Following the experiments, the spacecraft briefly pulled together again, this time with the Soyuz acting as the active vehicle. While ultimately successful, the second docking was more difficult than had been expected, apparently due in large part to difficulty on the Apollo side with the optical alignment sight. Sunlight reflecting off Soyuz during the docking procedure obscured the Americans' view, limiting the sight's usefulness. As a result, the Apollo's skewed attitude placed a great deal of strain on the Soyuz docking mechanism, but Leonov was still able to bring the two together, definitively demonstrating the docking module's usefulness from either side of the project's technology continuum.[13]

Soyuz 19 then bid farewell to Apollo, and returned to earth two days later, on July 21. The landing was televised live—another first-ever feat of openness for the Soviets—in both the United States and the USSR. For Americans accustomed to seeing the Apollos float under their three balloonlike parachutes to what looked like a graceful plop into the Pacific, the Soviet landing held some startling surprises.

Flying out of the sky under a single large red-and-white-striped parachute that looked for all the world like an old lady's bathing cap, the squat landing capsule rushed headlong toward the earth, finally hitting it with a fearful-looking impact that kicked up clouds of dust and debris that completely shrouded the spacecraft. Then came a feeling of relief as the cosmonauts exited the craft, smiling and waving to the cameras.

A much more familiar sight followed: the Soviet mission control engineers, politely clapping and smiling, looked very much like their American counterparts.[14]

The Apollo Victory Lap

The last Apollo remained in orbit for three more days, conducting experiments designed individually to further various aspects of space science and collectively to mute criticism of ASTP as a purely political stunt lacking in scientific value. That much of the criticism had come from outside the scientific community, and largely from the political arena, made little difference to NASA, whose highest ambitions had almost always been held hostage to the favors of the national political leadership and the mood of the people.[15]

And then, after its final nine days in space, the long flight of Apollo was over. Starting in tragedy, moving to triumph, and finally pointing the way to humanity's last, best hope for earthly survival and the start of the long reach into the far heavens, Apollo came home to earth on July 24, 1975. Stafford, Slayton, and Brand splashed down in the Pacific,

330 miles northwest of Hawaii, and were retrieved by the USS *New Orleans.*

The astronauts appeared fit and well as they exited the spacecraft, standing and waving in unison on the deck of the recovery ship. But their happy demeanor was in reality one final demonstration of the courage that had typified the astronaut corps from the very beginning.

During their descent, at an altitude of 23,000 feet, the astronauts noticed a brownish yellow gas entering the spacecraft. The gas quickly became overpowering, and Vance Brand had passed out by the time his fellow crew members were able to clamp an oxygen mask on him, pulling on their own at the same time. Brand recovered consciousness before the ship hit the water, but all three had inhaled a substantial amount of the mysterious substance. The mishap would cost them five days at the Tripler Army Medical Center in Honolulu, to recover from inflammation of their lungs.[16]

Subsequent investigation indicated that the astronauts had forgotten to deactivate the craft's thruster system during reentry, thereby allowing the toxic rocket propellant nitrogen tetroxide to seep into the cabin. At a news conference in Washington, D.C., in August, Brand took responsibility for failing to activate the two switches that would have shut the system down. But Tom Stafford spread the blame among all three crew members, noting that neither he nor Slayton had noticed that the switches had not been activated, either. NASA investigators also made note of an unexplained squeal in the communications system during the descent, which they felt might have distracted the crew at the crucial moment the switches should have been thrown.

All three astronauts recovered from the effects of inhaling the gas, but for Deke Slayton the incident led to another encounter with the doctors. During a careful examination of X rays they'd made prior to the flight, made necessary by their investigation into the effects of the incident, doctors found a small lesion on Slayton's left lung. It was removed during an operation in Houston at the end of August, and proved benign. Slayton recovered quickly and joined his fellow space travelers in Moscow in mid-September for a joint tour of the Soviet Union, followed by a similar journey through the United States a month later.[17]

When Vance Brand had taken the blame for the switch mishap, he had demonstrated the courage for which the astronauts and their predecessors were so enthusiastically cheered during public relations appearances such as the joint tours. In many respects, his position at the center of the incident seemed more bad luck than missed assignment, and he had had his share of bad luck throughout the mission. Back in early July, as the crew put Apollo through its final preflight tests, they discovered a leaky valve in one of the astronauts' spacesuits—Brand's. And during the potentially life-threatening descent, he had been the only member of the crew to lose consciousness. But none of the bad luck could overshadow the good fortune of having taken the flight, or its achievements. And Brand would go on to command several flights of the space shuttle in the space program's next era.

Tom Stafford's role in the mission had frequently been as much diplomatic as technical; a prime reason for his selection as commander of the Apollo half of ASTP was his previous acquaintance with various cosmonauts and Russian space officials. Prior to the flight, back in June, NASA was receiving heavy criticism and questions from some corners of the Senate about the Soviets' technical abilities and the resultant potential danger to the safety of the astronauts. Given his experience, stature, and conviction, and his position as the ASTP commander about to wager his very life on the flight's success, Stafford was NASA's most authoritative defender. During the White House celebration of the mission's success, President Ford promoted Stafford from brigadier general to major general, putting him at a rank equal to that of his international colleague Alexei Leonov, who had also been promoted to major general upon his return to earth. Having done as much as anyone to further the efforts of America in space, Stafford announced at the end of August that he was leaving the astronaut corps on November 1, to return to active duty with the U.S. Air Force.

And Deke Slayton, who had finally gotten his chance to fly in space, epitomized best of all the mission's meaning and accomplishment. In a news conference just prior to the surgery he would undergo to eliminate the lesion in his lung, he said he considered himself lucky that the tumor had been discovered while it was still small, and after the Apollo-Soyuz flight had been completed. With the perspective afforded by having been present at the program's creation, with the first flights of Mercury and Gemini, having been present at the *Apollo 1* disaster, assigning crews to the Apollo missions, and having at last been able to soar himself into the heavens, Slayton was able to appreciate the spirit of America's first steps into space as well as their practical significance. The description of his experience aboard Apollo during ASTP, published in the 1994 memoir he coauthored with Alan Shepard, is as moving and eloquent an argument for humanity's continued exploration of space as any yet written.

The End of the Apollo Era

Because of their unique position of honor in the public imagination, the initial groups of astronauts were the individuals most capable of articulating NASA's goals and ambitions. As the veterans began to leave the agency in the 1970s, their absence emboldened critics of the space program's goals, its administration, and particularly its cost.

Few of the politicians decrying the nation's expenditures on space exploration seemed to realize the irony of their arguments. The United States had throughout the 1960s been continuously and disastrously willing to commit ever-increasing amounts of troops and financial aid to the ever-worsening Vietnam War, even though these steps consistently brought results that were ever less satisfying. At the same time, the achievements of the space program, with the awful exception of *Apollo 1*, had been increasingly positive and evident throughout the decade.

Of course, by the time of ASTP, criticizing the space program had become at least acceptable, if not entirely fashionable. The euphoria of the race to the moon and the subsequent landings had begun to fade, largely due to the failure of anyone in a leadership position to articulate a new goal worthy of Kennedy's initial challenge. The reason for such failure seems twofold: first, there was the preoccupation of the nation's political leadership with other pressing issues, and second, there was a change in the national attitude about the program's currency, as the era it had most vibrantly represented came to an obvious close.

There were certainly issues other than cooperation in space that were more important to the world's political leaders at the time. During Nixon's first summit with the Russians, for example, at which he signed the agreement that led to ASTP, other items on the agenda included the possible overt involvement of the Soviet Union in the Vietnam War, and the limiting of the two superpowers' arsenal of nuclear weapons. Discussion of how to avoid war, nuclear or otherwise, was understandably the leaders' top priority.[18]

And yet, in retrospect the space agreement seems something of a missed chance to achieve a lasting positive relationship between the two nations, if only in regard to the space effort; the consequences might have been far-reaching if the opportunity had been better exploited.

Astute and authoritative when discussing the Soviet Union, Nixon did not seem to think much of ASTP's potential to make a lasting difference in the U.S.-Soviet relationship. In all the writing he did following his departure from the presidency, including his autobiography, he gives the mission scant mention. While this may be attributed to the fact that his administration did not survive to see the agreement's denouement, it is perhaps significant that his successor, Gerald Ford, who spoke at length with the crew during the mission and had the happy task of welcoming the astronauts back to earth upon their return, mentions the flight only elliptically in his own memoirs, even as he ascribes it to Nixon as one of the former president's finest achievements.[19]

The practical accomplishments of the Apollo program, and of the agency that had imagined, designed, and implemented it, had been great in number and lasting in significance. But at the end, with the space shuttle still under development and several years away and no more Apollo missions to fly, there was a desperate need in an America besieged by doubt and loss to invoke the poetry of the Apollo legacy. The Apollo-Soyuz Test Project had been the proud last issue of the old adventurous idea that somehow the reach into space would lead the country to grasp new solutions to its persistent problems. When it was finished, America could take pride that it had reached out to an old adversary to shake hands across the heavens (actually, high above Metz, France, as the newly linked Apollo and Soyuz craft drifted over the city on the mission's second day). Like the cowboys of 1950s American westerns, having completed its duty and leaving peace in its wake, Apollo was to ride gloriously off into the sunset.

11

The 1970s: Journeys Without and Within

Sadly, the sun was to set as well on the United States in space for the remainder of the decade. As a result, the meaning and message of Apollo, the bearer of the best instincts of its time, were to fall dormant as the country entered a period of troubled reflection about the era that had just come to an end.

As it frequently had in the past, NASA's development during the late 1970s closely followed the nation's. By the time the last Apollo spacecraft splashed down in the Pacific in July 1975, the country was finally free of the Vietnam War, but had as a result to live with the fact that it had failed at arms for the first time in its history. The loss of life and loss of honor were most galling for two particular groups of people: those who had fought in World War II, and those who were employed in the military and related industries. There was a certain amount of disgust among those groups for the way the conflict had been conducted politically, and the conclusion that the war had been lost by failures of political leadership as much as any other factor was gradually adopted by a good portion of the population.[1]

The net effect of disillusionment with the war was a national malaise, a feeling of idealism gone awry by its progression to an unnatural conclusion. America was at once embarrassed by and ambivalent about Vietnam, and eager to leave it and its era behind.

The Gifts of Apollo

In its final flight, the Apollo program had given the country one last gift that, in its hope for the future, may have been the series' most idealistic accomplishment of all. The joint mission that brought American astronauts Stafford, Slayton and Brand together with the USSR's Leonov and Kubasov was a great symbolic epitaph for Apollo and for the cycle of American history that was the 1960s and early 1970s. ASTP looked far into the future and envisioned some form of peace among the world's superpowers, once the chaos of competition—over space, nuclear weapons, regional influences, and all the other points of contention—subsided enough for reasonable discussion to take place and cooperative work to begin.

The timing of the mission was in some measure ironic, as it came less than a year after the other great disillusionment of the era, beyond the Vietnam War, had run its course. After bringing the war to a close and opening the door to cooperation with the other great superpowers, Richard Nixon's involvement in Watergate had wrecked his presidency and forced him to resign on August 9, 1974.

Nixon had been elected to a second term as president less than two years earlier by an astonishing 60.8 percent of the popular vote. He received more than 47 million votes in 1972, more than any other presidential candidate up to that time, and over the course of his three presidential campaigns, he received a total of more than 113 million votes.[2]

He resigned after more than a year and a half of increasingly astonishing revelations about the actions of his campaign committee, those of his staff, and his own conduct while in office. As with the war, the great numbers of people who had supported the president and his administration with their votes and their gradually waning faith in his ability to maintain his office were left at the end with a feeling of ambivalence, and were perhaps relieved that the Nixon years, for better or worse, were over.

Despite his influential role in the mission's formative stages and his involvement with so many previous historic moments in the program's past, the former president had fallen so far out of favor by the time of the flight that he was not invited to attend the final Apollo launch.

By the time of ASTP in 1975, there had been an almost continual stream of great events in America. Popular public figures had abruptly vanished, sometimes violently, from the national political arena, and the nation's social discourse had changed radically since the 1950s and the first rumblings of the nascent American space program. There had been great achievements, of which the most obvious and enduring in the national memory was the *Apollo 11* trip to the moon; there had also been at least a few equally obvious failures, which most of the citizenry seemed to prefer to forget.

Largely determining which events the public would be allowed to forget and those that would remain in its daily discourse was the nation's news media, which was in perhaps its greatest modern ascendancy during the late 1960s and early 1970s. Given the number and the lasting importance of the events it had to cover during that period, the press quite logically grew in importance, and by generally acquitting itself well with the public, it also grew in credibility and aggressiveness.

NASA's press coverage had long been favorable, and contributed to some degree to the agency's success. In some ways the exploration of space has always represented a sort of case study of the American democracy in action, as funding and political support for U.S. space activities has nearly always reflected the level of interest of the population as a whole. The Mercury, Gemini, and Apollo programs that eventually placed their fellow Americans on the moon were supported by the American people by virtue of their watching the events of those programs on television, reading about the personalities and the systems involved, and discussing the hopes and dreams that going to the moon represented.

Once the conquest of the moon had been achieved, those hopes and dreams seemed fulfilled. The memory of the late President Kennedy, the first and perhaps the only political leader to translate the space program's goals into an activity of great national interest, had been honored, and there were precious few new objectives—with the exception of the symbolically important ASTP—that seemed worthy of the same sort of grand rhetorical flourish or the same degree of emotional involvement on the part of the public.[3]

After Vietnam and Watergate and the tumult of their era, and following its own almost continual activity during the 1960s and early 1970s, the U.S. space program entered a long interregnum from 1975 to 1981, that echoed the tenor of the times. Much like the formality of a funeral for an elderly, long-suffering relative, a mood of mourning and introspection took hold of the country in the mid-1970s, and a sense of anticipation grew up about what might lay in store once the grief had passed.

12

Echoes: The Shuttle Era and Beyond

At 7:00 A.M. Eastern standard time, Sunday, April 12, 1981, after an absence of more than five and a half years, America resumed the business of putting its citizens into space.

With a violent blast, the space shuttle *Columbia*—the most complex spacecraft yet built—lifted off launch pad 39A at Cape Canaveral, Florida, with astronauts John Young and Robert Crippen aboard.

Young, the flight's commander, was an icon of NASA's past glories. He'd joined the astronaut corps in 1962, as one of the second group of astronauts selected by NASA, and flew the first manned Gemini flight, *Gemini 3*, with Gus Grissom in March 1965. He then commanded *Gemini 10* in July 1966, during which Michael Collins (who would later orbit the moon during *Apollo 11*) performed two successful extravehicular activities (EVAs).

Young had landed on the moon in 1972; he and fellow *Apollo 16* crewman Charlie Duke conducted three moonwalks totaling more than twenty hours before their return to earth. And as part of the *Apollo 10* crew in 1969, he had circled the moon just three months prior to the first landing.

Crippen, a test pilot whose flight aboard *Columbia* marked the end of nearly twelve years of waiting to fly in space, had first arrived at NASA in that golden year of 1969.

But this was a new era. About the only direct similarity between the massive winged bird that was about to lift America back into the heavens and the capsules of previous years was the echo of the name *Columbia*, which the nostalgia-minded would immediately recognize as the name of the *Apollo 11* command module.

The new vehicle was enormously complex compared to its moonshot ancestors. The Mercury, Gemini, and Apollo craft were all state-of-the-art in their day, but each outlived its usefulness at about the same time that its replacement came along. Even by the time of the joint Apollo-Soyuz mission of 1975, the technology that would be integrated into the shuttle had already made that which had preceded it seem prosaic by comparison. The goals of the new era of space exploration were completely different from those of the moon-landing days, and the systems, design, and management of the new vehicles starkly reflected the shift.

The country was itself utterly changed since the last Apollo had splashed down in the Pacific. An entirely new mood had taken hold in the nation, and the shuttle epitomized the new attitude in both its best intentions and in its most grievous shortcomings.

For everyone associated with the program, the interval between the last Apollo and the day that Young and Crippen were to fly the inaugural shuttle mission had been a long wait. Public interest in space exploration had long since moved on from the glory days of NASA's lunar exploits, and the agency's ability to communicate the shuttle's purpose and value was not on a par with its earlier promotional efforts—likely because the space race and John F. Kennedy's end-of-the-decade deadline for a first landing on the moon provided a much more logical and appealing story than the earth orbit "space transportation system."

Great Expectations

Early press coverage of the shuttle was often vague and misleading, and it helped to fuel unrealistic expectations of how fast the program was likely to achieve its goals. A 1978 *Life* magazine photo of the shuttle *Enterprise*, for example, carried a caption that promised no less for the reusable orbiting "spaceplane" than its ability to "pioneer the age of space colonization." The short description also noted that the shuttle's first liftoff was scheduled for early 1979.[1]

Of course, "space colonization" had already been pioneered by the American *Skylab* and more significantly—and successfully—by the Soviets throughout the 1970s. Devotion to its space station program had nearly caused a problem for the Soviets during the ASTP flight, when *Soyuz 18* began a two-month mission that briefly overlapped with the joint Apollo-Soyuz project. NASA's engineers worried that the two missions might interfere with each other, or that they might overburden Soviet resources on the ground, but the Soviets insisted that there would be no conflict because they would use two separate ground control teams. As it worked out, both ASTP and *Soyuz 18* flew as planned, the latter docking successfully with the *Salyut 4* space station, its two-man crew conducting a variety of experiments during its stay. For all its success, the Soviet space station mission had its dire moments; the innards of the craft broke out in a grotesque green mold, and cosmonauts Pyotr Klimuk and Vitali Sevastyanov endured a great deal of discomfort while waiting for their mission to end. Despite their pleas for an early return to earth, the Soviet space hierarchy insisted they stay until the end of the scheduled time, to keep up the appearance that all was well while the ASTP mission progressed.[2]

An earlier attempt at the same mission had ended with the first human launch abort, when cosmonauts Vasili Lazarev and Oleg Makarov survived a rocket failure on April 5, 1975. The retro-rockets on their Soyuz capsule propelled them some nine hundred miles from the launch site, pushing them out of danger from the exploding rocket but providing them a hellishly short trip into space and back, and leaving them just short of the border between the USSR and China. Both crew members were seriously injured, but they were located and saved in a difficult rescue.[3]

Despite their troubles, the Soviets made impressive gains in their space station program throughout the 1970s and into the early 1980s, continually increasing both the length of individual stays in space and their knowledge of the effects such long-duration spaceflight might have on the human body. They also continued to propagate the dark side of their success, as they had in the early years, with clumsy boasting, misinformation, and bald propaganda tainting their otherwise admirable inclusion of foreign researchers in their space efforts.

Early Years of the Space Shuttle

As its name implies, the shuttle was first envisioned by NASA as a means of transportation, originally intended to shuttle astronauts, equipment, and supplies from the earth to and from an American space station in earth orbit. The agency's plans for a continuous presence in space were severely curtailed, however, by cutbacks in the federal budget even before the last lunar landings were completed.

Plans of grander things, such as an inhabited lunar colony or astronauts landing on Mars, were also shelved in the early 1970s, although they seem to have a life of their own, and have periodically cropped up and been killed off several times in the intervening decades.

Because of his seminal role in reining in NASA's farthest-flung plans for the 1970s and beyond, Richard Nixon is often cited, as his biographer Tom Wicker notes, as "the president who set in motion the long decline of the America space program."[4] In all fairness, however, Nixon seems no more or less guilty than any of the presidents who have followed him in failing to articulate some grand national purpose for the space program. The huge cost of sending human beings safely beyond earth's orbit requires committed political leadership and the overriding approval of the American people. Thus the budgetary constraints that the Nixon administration cited as a primary reason for not supporting such missions in the early 1970s were echoed in the Clinton administration's decision in early 1998 not to endorse funding for any efforts to land humans on the moon or on Mars.[5]

Even without a space station to go to, the shuttle is in itself an impressive destination. The crowds waiting in the early morning sun for that first launch in April 1981 could hardly fail to appreciate the craft's sleek aerodynamic design or its size compared to earlier spacecraft. The shuttle orbiter is over 122 feet long and nearly 59 feet high, with a wingspan of 78.2 feet and a 900–square-foot cargo bay.[6]

The complete system prior to launch consists of the airplanelike reusable shuttle orbiter, a massive external fuel tank (at 154 feet long and 27.5 feet in diameter, it is itself the size of a 747), and two reusable solid-fuel rocket boosters (SRBs). At launch, the external tank feeds a mix of liquid oxygen and liquid hydrogen to the orbiter's three main engines at the rate of 1,122 pounds of propellant per second, while the SRBs kick in after the main engines and lift the shuttle off the launch pad. Responsible for seeing the orbiter through the first part of its journey, to an altitude of about thirty miles, the SRBs provide more than 5 million pounds of thrust.[7]

Rush to Orbit

In contrast to the obvious grandeur of the enormous, complex machine sitting on the launch pad, about to take Young and Crippen into orbit and return the United States to space for the first time in nearly six years, there were fundamental flaws in the financial assumptions NASA was projecting for the shuttle program's future costs, and in the expectations of the Reagan administration and the U.S. Congress. Thanks to inflation and technical delays, the program's projected cost of $5.2 billion had reached $10 billion by the time of the first launch. In addition to *Columbia*, three more shuttles—*Challenger, Discovery*, and *Atlantis*—were on the way at a cost of more than $500 million each.[8]

From the very beginning, the high cost of the shuttle program focused intense pressure on NASA to pay its own way as much as possible, generating revenue by ferrying satellites into earth orbit for paying customers. There was no question that the revenue could be quite substantial; as one of the shuttle's "primary users," as the jargon of the day referred to them, the Defense Department had already spent $1 billion in shuttle-related activities prior to the first launch.[9]

But the price of too heavy an emphasis on the shuttle's commercial applications was an utterly unrealistic view of even the best-case prospects for the program's financial outlook. In order to increase the shuttle's price-to-performance ratio, the agency would have to undertake as many flights as possible each year. As a result, just prior to the first launch, NASA was projecting a total of between five hundred and six hundred shuttle flights from the start of the program through the end of the 1990s.[10] The plan in April 1981 estimated a cost per mission in the range of $35 million to $40 million in 1981 dollars, with $5 million per flight recouped from paying customers.[11]

A schedule as hectic as the one proposed seemed bound to create logistical problems, perhaps endangering the mission or even jeopardizing the safety of the crew and the vehicle. But by its nature, the shuttle was designed as an easier way into space, less costly per flight and more productive in material terms than its predecessors. Thus the initial planning, development, and forecast of the shuttle's first few years represented a radically different approach from that employed in the Mercury, Gemini, and Apollo programs. Despite its prestige as NASA's crowning achievement in the first era of space exploration, Apollo faced particularly harsh comparison to the shuttle in the early to mid-1980s. Apollo had cost $24 billion in 1962 dollars, or $48 billion in 1988 dollars. It certainly promised far less tangible rewards than the shuttle program, but actually delivered a great number of technologies, systems, and operational methods that have since been adapted for commercial use. And all material benefits aside, there is little question of Apollo's ultimate scientific value; on that basis alone it was an enormous bargain.[12]

A Good Beginning

While the public mulled the relative practical merits of the nation's return to space, the first shuttle flight went smoothly. Young and Crippen lifted off with great fanfare, spent more than two days in orbit, and returned safely with minimal damage to *Columbia*, which suffered the loss of or damage to about 160 of the ceramic tiles designed to protect it from the heat of reentry into the earth's atmosphere. Theirs was the first test flight of the shuttle to fly in space, and the new spacecraft performed admirably well. It was an excellent proving flight, and a good start for the program.[13]

One aspect of the mission that received a great deal of press attention at the time was the fact that Young and Crippen had several means of escape if something went wrong at launch or during the flight. Much was made of the ejection seats that would presumably vault them to safety if an accident occurred on the pad or just after launch.

But while the escape idea was interesting, it was also destined to be short-lived. Aptly representing the perspective of the Mercury-Gemini-Apollo-era NASA, Young's friend and fellow *Gemini 10* crew member Michael Collins pointed out the fragility of the shuttle's safety precautions shortly before *Columbia*'s first launch.

> Once the two gigantic solid rocket boosters ignite, the shuttle is utterly dependent on them, with no escape rockets to pull it free in case of danger. On the first flights, the two-man crew will be provided ejection seats, but when the crew grows to four or seven, the ejection seats will be removed, and from then on the solids simply must not fail.[14]

The early test flights continued with the next three missions, ending with *Columbia*'s fourth flight in June and July 1982. Minor problems cropped up along the way—the most serious was a fuel cell failure that cut the second mission from five days to three—but the large majority of the test program's objectives were achieved.

Following the test program, the first "operational" shuttle flight took place in November 1982. ASTP veteran Vance Brand was commander of *Columbia*'s four-man crew (each test mission had carried only two crew members), and the first test of the orbiter's commercial viability went well. *Columbia* performed flawlessly in deploying the mission's primary payload, two commercial communications satellites. The only disappointment of the five-day mission occurred when a malfunction in the $2.1 million extravehicular mobility unit (EMU) space suit forced the cancellation of the first scheduled spacewalk of the shuttle program.[15]

That goal was achieved by mission specialists Donald H. Peterson and F. Story Musgrave on the next shuttle flight, in April, 1983—the first flight of the *Challenger.* Photos of the two astronauts tethered to the huge open cargo bay adorned the front page of newspapers across the nation, and accounts of the planning, accomplishment, and aftermath of their extended extravehicular activity (EVA) of four-plus hours led television and radio newscasts for several days. It was the first American spacewalk since 1974.[16]

The New Astronaut

The inclusion of mission specialists and payload specialists as crew members is one of the shuttle's great advances on the Mercury-Gemini-Apollo years. The complexity of the shuttles' systems and equipment, the orbiters' larger work area, and the commercial nature of many of the tasks crew members must perform during a given flight were all part of the original impetus for NASA to expand shuttle crews to include nonastronauts.

The traditional duties of launch, insertion into orbit, deorbit, and landing continue to be the responsibility of astronauts—the commander and pilot. Added duties related to the work the orbiter must accomplish during the trip, however, are portioned out to the mission specialists, who are responsible for the proper handling and maintenance of payloads and the systems and equipment the shuttle employs for activities such as launching and retrieving satellites and conducting spacewalks. Most mission specialists are NASA employees who have been specially trained to operate the vehicle's complex systems.

Payload specialists, as the name implies, are usually nonastronaut employees of an agency or company that has bought a spot for its payload on a given shuttle flight. In cases where a payload is owned by NASA or the Department of Defense, the payload specialists may be employees of the space agency or the military, and the crew in that case may more accurately echo the composition of the earliest groups of astronauts in experience and background. Generally, however, the commercial aspects of the shuttle program have ensured a trip into space for a larger and more diverse population of space travelers.[17]

First American Woman in Space

In June 1983, as NASA celebrated its twenty-fifth anniversary, the equal opportunity of the new approach resulted in the first flight of an American woman in space. Dr. Sally K. Ride, a physicist who began her astronaut training in 1978, played an instrumental role in the seventh shuttle mission. She and fellow mission specialists John Fabian and Norman Thagard operated the spacecraft's fifty-foot robotic arm (also known, officially, as the remote manipulator system or RMS) to retrieve and release the shuttle pallet satellite (SPS), proving the device's abilities for later missions.

The flight demonstrated the best instincts of the early years of the shuttle program in many ways. In addition to its milestone value for women hoping to fly in space one day, the mission was also indicative of the program's new international emphasis. The RMS "arm" that Ride and her crewmates used to capture the little SPS artificial moon was a Canadian innovation, and the satellite itself was manufactured in West Germany. At the conclusion of the flight, the planned landing at the Kennedy Space Center was scrubbed due to poor weather conditions, and the landing took place at Edwards Air Force base in California instead—a clear demonstration of the flexibility of the program and versatility of the vehicle, since such weather conditions likely would have wreaked havoc with the missions of the Mercury-Gemini-Apollo era.[18]

Once the gender barrier had been broken, similar milestones followed in rapid succession. On the eighth shuttle mission, in August and September 1983, the *Challenger* successfully achieved the first night launch and first night landing, and mission specialist Guion S. Bluford Jr. became the first African American to fly in space. Ulf Merbold of Germany became the first representative of the European Space Agency (ESA) to fly on the shuttle during mission nine.

Mission specialists Bruce McCandless and Robert Stewart were the first to make untethered spacewalks by using the manned maneuvering unit (MMU) on the tenth shuttle flight in February 1984. At more than five hours, the excursion of the free-floating dual spacewalkers represented an advance of almost inconceivable magnitude over the short, strenuous efforts of their earliest counterparts, who had conducted the first EVAs just two decades earlier.[19]

Noting the singular nature of the experience that McCandless and Stewart shared as they floated 175 miles above the earth, mission commander Vance Brand joked, "They call each other Flash Gordon and Buck Rogers." The reference to the science fiction characters made famous in 1930s Saturday morning movie serials gave journalists around the world a perfect hook for their coverage of the event, and revealed a humorous dimension of the astronaut personality that had seemed oddly missing for a long while. Perhaps appropriately, the flight was the first of the shuttle era to end with a landing at the Kennedy Space Center.

Sadly, the same mission also saw the first major failures of the shuttle delivery system, as the two communications satellites that were its primary payloads failed to achieve orbit after they were deployed.[20]

Orbital Repairs

Two months later, during the eleventh shuttle mission, another major advance was made when the shuttle chased down, caught, and repaired the *Solar Maximum* satellite. Designed to study and photograph solar flares, *"Solar Max"* was launched in February 1980. Toward the end of its first year in orbit, the $325 million satellite suffered serious failures in its onboard electronics that threatened to render it useless. Using the MMU units tested on the previous flight, the *Challenger* astronauts replaced key parts of the satellite's electronics during their April 1984 mission, achieving the first in-orbit satellite repair and demonstrating the shuttle's enormous promise for future repair work.[21]

The shuttle *Discovery* launched on its maiden space voyage on August 30, 1984, following the first pad abort of the program, on June 26, when the orbiter's onboard computer sensed something wrong with one of its engines just four seconds before launch. Following the replacement of the engine, a third launch attempt on August 29 was scrubbed because of a software problem. To counteract the delays and preserve the launch schedule for future missions, payloads from the next scheduled mission were added to *Discovery*'s cargo manifest.[22]

Discovery also flew the first shuttle mission devoted solely to delivering payloads for the Department of Defense, in January 1985. Given its long traditions of civilian leadership and a climate of open communication about its activities, NASA was perceived by the media and the public as suddenly taking a secretive turn toward the military. Anyone familiar with the shuttle program's long incubation throughout the 1970s knew better: military involvement with the shuttle was not a particularly new development, and it was certainly less sinister than it may have seemed. As a major client of the space transportation system, with frequent payloads and a universally accepted, high-priority role in protecting the nation's interests worldwide, the Department of Defense gave vital support to the shuttle program in its early years, when its usefulness and credibility were most severely questioned. At the end of the 1970s, when cost overruns and technical delays threatened future shuttle development, the Pentagon bailed NASA out of its predicament by convincing President Jimmy Carter to increase funding for the program.[23]

Once the shuttle was operational, its classified flights returned the favor in both practical and visionary ways. In addition to the obvious benefit of providing the military with a path to orbit that could be tightly cloaked in secrecy, the shuttle's ability to visit space so frequently also gave the Reagan administration's Strategic Defense Initiative (SDI) whatever credence it might have had. The so-called Star Wars concept envisioned orbiting laser battle stations as part of a defensive shield that could protect the United States from nuclear attack. It was an idea that Ronald Reagan strongly supported throughout his two terms as president, and a key component of his approach to arms control negotiations with the Soviet Union.[24]

Perhaps the most impressive achievement of the first half decade of the shuttle program was the relative ease that marked the frequent flights. Even though NASA did not achieve the harried, unrealistic pace that early planners had envisioned, the four shuttle orbiters (*Atlantis* launched on its first mission in October 1985) flew often and accumulated an impressive string of accomplishments that greatly advanced space travel and science, and particularly space commerce. Coupled with the technology spinoffs of the earlier programs, the advances of the shuttle era have clearly signaled a new age, steeped in computer technology and heavily reliant on the development of next-generation communications systems.

Unspeakable Loss: The *Challenger* Disaster

Five years and twenty-four flights into the shuttle era, space travel seemed less dramatic than it had at any other time in the history of the U.S. program. Media coverage of launches and in-flight activities lessened, with a resulting drop in public awareness of individual missions and of the program as a whole.

Then, just as space travel began to seem prosaic, the explosion of the space shuttle *Challenger* seared its way into the national consciousness, indelibly refuting any thoughts that the trip would be easy or without pain.

Just as its computerized systems are intricately programmed to guide massive spacecraft into delicate flight, NASA in the early 1980s was itself programmed to pursue success, a success increasingly defined less by the human elements of national faith and pride than by the economic strictures and technological precisions of timely flight and properly delivered payloads.

After a series of delays, *Challenger* lifted off the newly renovated pad 39B at the Kennedy Space Center at 11:38 A.M. Eastern standard time on January 28, 1986. The last vehicle to launch from the site had been the Apollo portion of the Apollo-Soyuz Test Project in 1975.

Seventy-three seconds into the flight, a fault in a rubber O-ring on one of the solid rocket boosters caused the SRB to spew its fiery mix of aluminum, aluminum perchlorate, and iron-oxide onto the huge external fuel tank, igniting its liquid oxygen and liquid hydrogen and causing a massive explosion that destroyed the orbiter and killed the seven members of the *Challenger* crew.

The SRBs themselves remained intact for about a minute more, until ground controllers programmed them to self-destruct. It was unclear at the time if the crew had survived the initial explosion, but later investigation indicated that at least some crew members had probably survived and may have been conscious during the nine-mile, two-and-a-half-minute fall to the surface of the Atlantic, where they were killed when the still-intact crew compartment impacted the water at an estimated speed of two hundred miles per hour.[25]

Francis Scobee was commander of the *Challenger*; he was joined on the mission by pilot Michael Smith, mission specialists Judith Resnick, Ellison Onizuka, and Ronald McNair, payload specialist Gregory Jarvis, and Christa McAuliffe, who had been selected from a pool of 11,000 applicants to be the first "Teacher in Space" as part of NASA's commitment to providing opportunities for private citizens to fly in space.[26]

As part of the Teacher in Space project, classes of schoolchildren across the nation were watching the shuttle launch when the fatal accident occurred.

The Investigation

Shortly after the accident, President Reagan empaneled an investigative commission headed by William Rogers, former secretary of state in the Nixon administration and attorney general during the presidency of Dwight Eisenhower. The Rogers Commission also included astronauts Neil Armstrong (who had retired from NASA shortly after *Apollo 11*) and Sally Ride, several aerospace executives and academics, and Charles (Chuck) Yeager, the test pilot pioneer who had been the first human being to fly faster than the speed of sound.

The commission presented its final report to the president on June 9, just a little more than four months after the accident. Word quickly leaked to the press that harsh criticism of NASA by commission member Richard Feynman, the Nobel Prize–winning physicist at the California Institute of Technology, had been excised or toned down in the final text of the report.

Even in its apparently sanitized final form, the Rogers report was severely critical of NASA. The agency portrayed by the commission in its sternest admonitions is the nightmare runaway bureaucracy of a sort of definitive anti-1980s cautionary tale. While tipping its hat to past glories and conveying a final judgment that the agency was still worthy of continued recognition as a "symbol of national pride and technological leadership," the commission's overall conclusions left little doubt that NASA had utterly lost its way since the glory days of the Apollo program.

The vast enterprise that had epitomized the nation's best instincts in the 1960s, uniting some 400,000 individuals scattered throughout its own operations, the academic community, and thousands of companies across the United States, had apparently devolved into a bureaucracy so futile that it could inadvertently kill seven astronauts not by unforeseen risks or unavoidable human error, but by "management isolation" and "a lack of communication."[27]

Most damning of all was the conclusion that NASA managers had ignored warnings that the accident was likely to happen. Engineers at Thiokol Corporation, manufacturer of the SRBs and the O-rings that were part of them, had questioned the likely effect of cold weather on the O-rings after discovering that the rings on SRBs recovered after previous launches had suffered severe damage. The engineers' concerns were dismissed by Thiokol's management, which was under pressure from NASA management to stick to the launch schedule.

In several instances prior to the loss of *Challenger*, the calculated decision to favor the bottom line over the advice of the engineers had had no dire consequences. Shuttles were launched, the O-rings held well enough despite the damage, and the resulting conventional wisdom dictated that nothing was seriously enough wrong to warrant the involvement of senior NASA management.[28] But in testimony before the commission, officials from shuttle manufacturer Rockwell International recalled that they had warned NASA that they could not ensure a safe launch because of the sheets of ice that covered various parts of the launch facility.[29]

As the investigation progressed, President Reagan expressed strong support for NASA and encouraged a quick return to space as soon as the conditions that had led to the disaster were identified and corrected. His initial comments, delivered in lieu of his scheduled State of the Union address on the evening of the accident, were indicative of his support. Addressing the children who had witnessed the explosion, the president explained that the accident had been "part of the process of exploration and discovery . . . The future doesn't belong to the fainthearted; it belongs to the brave. The *Challenger* crew was pulling us into the future, and we'll continue to follow them."[30] Schedules slavishly adhered to and corners cut in the name of efficiency have long been cited as crucial components of the decision-making process that led to the loss of *Challenger.* That NASA initially failed to grasp the totality of that loss, and the need for a change in attitude toward its purpose and its public, was evident in the months following the accident.

In April 1986, less than three months after the disaster and more than two weeks before the first of the *Challenger* crew was laid to rest, the agency released a tentative schedule of future shuttle flights: four for 1987, twelve in 1988. Perhaps even more chilling than these delusions of technological grandeur, even before the first human remains were interred, the schedule also made reference to an "orbiter 105," a *Challenger* replacement, even though there had not yet been any decision to build such a replacement.[31]

Floating a paper shuttle by an American public that had so recently been confronted with the specter of the real thing lying in pieces on the floor of the Atlantic, the only remaining physical link to the seven human beings who had been lost in the accident, betrayed the arrogance of an agency that once had been revered as the keeper of the nation's dreams.

Return to Flight

A far better attitude emerged within NASA and throughout the nation as the shock of the *Challenger* disaster began to recede into the past, even as it remains etched in the national psyche. Displaying echoes of the flexibility and resilience that once led it to the surface of the moon, NASA made substantial changes to its shuttle systems and equipment and, most important, to its approach to spaceflight. Management and personnel changes helped to transform the hubris of the immediate postaccident period into a quiet determination to learn the lessons of the failure and do everything possible to ensure that they would never be repeated.

Early plans notwithstanding, NASA's return to space took more than two and a half years. Frederick Hauck commanded *Discovery* in the shuttle's twenty-sixth mission, the first of the post-*Challenger* era, in late September and early October 1988.

In addition to a more rational flight schedule, the newest incarnation of the shuttle program also featured a renewed emphasis on space science. In the new era, several dedicated Spacelab life sciences missions featured an intense battery of tests to help determine how humans and animals adapt to weightlessness.

High-profile scientific payloads included the Venus radar mapper *Magellan* in May 1989 and the Jupiter probe *Galileo* in October of that year. In April 1990, on the shuttle's thirty-fifth mission, the Hubble space telescope was deployed, providing an "eye in space" for scientists and a new focus for public interest in space.

The new orbiter *Endeavor* made headlines with its first flight in May 1992, when its astronauts conducted four EVAs, including two record-setting spacewalks of eight and a half hours. Mission specialist Kathryn

Thornton took one of those extraterrestrial strolls, in the process setting a record for the longest EVA by a female astronaut.

On the fiftieth shuttle mission, in September 1992, science mission specialist Mae Jemison became the first African American woman to fly in space. The flight produced a treasure of richly symbolic milestones, including the first spaceflight of a married couple (payload commander Mark Lee and mission specialist N. Jan Davis) and the first shuttle flight for a Japanese citizen (payload specialist Mamoru Mohri of the National Space Development Agency of Japan).

Discovery's December 1992 flight marked the end of missions dedicated to the Department of Defense. The national-security secrecy that cloaked the first day's deployment of a classified DOD payload was lifted shortly after the cargo was delivered to space, and the remainder of the flight proceeded as usual.

At the close of 1993, the shuttle's value to the future of the U.S. space effort was dramatically demonstrated in a complex mission designed to complete the first servicing of the Hubble space telescope. Working in teams, the crew of the shuttle's fifty-ninth flight replaced several of the Hubble's scientific instruments and portions of its electronic subsystems during a series of five successive spacewalks over a period of more than thirty-five hours. Along the way, they also utilized the shuttle as a sort of space tugboat to boost the telescope to a slightly higher orbit of 321 nautical miles above the earth.[32]

As the program's achievements mounted and the passing years softened the shock of the traumatic last moments of *Challenger*, a measure of nostalgia for the long-ago glories of the Mercury, Gemini, and Apollo programs gradually began to emerge. The dissolution of the Soviet Union was for many Americans the definitive sign that a new age had dawned, and the symbolism of the sixtieth shuttle flight, in February 1994, was not lost on those who had lived through the space race and the superpower competition to be first on the moon. Mission specialist Sergei Krikalev of the Russian Space Agency was along for the ride on that shuttle mission—the first Russian cosmonaut to fly on an American shuttle.[33]

Cooperation between the United States and the Russian Republic would pay handsome dividends for both sides. A succession of U.S. astronauts visited the Russian space station *Mir*, giving the shuttle the opportunity to fulfill one of its original goals as a true space transportation system, shuttling passengers to and from their temporary home in space. Astronauts visiting *Mir* accumulated an impressive list of accomplishments; Shannon Lucid, for example, spent a record 188 days in space during her trip to the station in 1996.

Echoes Past and Future

Echoes of the past and new interest in the possibilities of the future were everywhere as the 1990s came to a close and the new millennium beckoned. The old dreams of returning to the lunar surface or figuring out some new way to touch down on Mars were excited anew by the exploits of two unmanned probes, the *Lunar Prospector* and the *Mars Pathfinder.*

A certain wistful nostalgia accompanied the launch of the *Lunar Prospector* in January 1998, as NASA began its first dedicated exploration of the moon since Gene Cernan and Jack Schmitt lifted off the lunar surface at the end of the *Apollo 17* mission back in 1972.

The tiny spacecraft produced evidence of water ice at the moon's north and south poles, and generated the first complete gravity map of the entire surface—an important reference for all future attempts at lunar exploration.

Most important, the *Lunar Prospector* again focused the public's attention on the idea of traveling to the moon, if even for a short while, and reaffirmed the enduring popular appeal of space science in general. Part of NASA's Discovery program of low-cost, carefully targeted planetary science missions, *Lunar Prospector* was also a bargain: the agency projected its total cost at $63 million.[34]

At $266 million, the *Mars Pathfinder* also turned out to be a startlingly good investment for the space agency. The mission produced a public relations windfall and generated unprecedented interest in the red planet, even outpacing the public clamor that surrounded the successful Mars exploration by the Viking probes in the mid-1970s.

Following its airbag-cushioned soft landing, the *Pathfinder* lander released the *Sojourner* rover, a small, flat robot about the size and dimensions of a child's toy wagon. While it could not live up to the overheated NASA rhetoric that lauded the little craft as "the robotic equivalent of Neil Armstrong," *Sojourner* did attract a great deal of affectionate attention, even to the point of becoming, as *Boston Globe* columnist Ellen Goodman put it, a sort of "national mascot." The mission's site on the World Wide Web attracted some 100 million visits during the first few days of *Sojourner's* stay on the Martian surface.[35]

A Hero Returns

The most sentimental space journey of all, however, belonged to John Glenn. Thirty-six years after becoming the first American in orbit and entering the final year of his four terms as a U.S. senator from the state of Ohio, the Mercury Seven veteran returned to spaceflight as a seventy-seven-year-old payload specialist on the space shuttle *Discovery*, on October 29, 1998. Glenn's new venture into space was the result of his vigorous lobbying of NASA and the National Institute on Aging—an effort in which he persisted for two years before prevailing.[36]

Despite the criticism of some who saw the flight as too rooted in publicity or too risky, Glenn made a compelling argument for himself as a stellar test subject for studying the similarities between the effects of weightlessness and the effects of aging. NASA had collected a massive amount of medical data about him during his Mercury Seven training and in the detailed physical exams that he and other former astronauts had allowed the space agency to perform over the years, and a new flight would provide an opportunity to use that information as a baseline for additional observations.

Less practical but no less compelling, the sentimental argument for the senator's return to space enjoyed wide appeal. Following his brief trip into orbit in 1962, Glenn was revered as a redeeming hero whose bravery had answered the early successes of the Soviet space program. To avoid the possibility of risking his life in a later mission, President Kennedy ordered NASA to keep Glenn on the ground—a fact that, despite their friendship, the astronaut discovered only long after the president's death. With the prospects of a new flight assignment fading and John and Robert Kennedy vigorously encouraging him to refocus his considerable talents on solving earthbound problems, Glenn retired from NASA in 1964 to make a run for the U.S. Senate. His first try at electoral politics was cut short by a freak accident, a slip in the bathroom that resulted in recurring dizziness and a long hospital stay.

A corporate career then intervened, until the presidential campaign of his friend Robert Kennedy inspired Glenn to return to politics. He and his wife, Annie, were in the Ambassador Hotel in Los Angeles, when Kennedy, celebrating his victory in the California primary, was shot, and Glenn later took on the difficult task of having to tell several of the Kennedy children that their father had passed away.

After an unsuccessful try in 1970, Glenn was elected to the U.S. Senate in 1974. He served four terms before he retired, shortly after completing his trip on the shuttle *Discovery.*

An obvious enthusiasm, positive attitude, and generous spirit had been the defining elements of John Glenn's personality since his first appearance in the public eye, when he made his Mercury Seven debut back in 1957. Embarking on his widely publicized return flight some forty-one years later, he suffered the glare of celebrity with the same mix of easy humor and fierce determination to succeed that had marked his earlier efforts.

One day in the spring of 1998, during a break in his training for the upcoming shuttle mission, Glenn received a visit from a friend: President Bill Clinton. Despite an injured knee and the worried looks of the Secret Service agents assigned to protect him, the president was persuaded by his impish septuagenarian pal to climb into the space shuttle simulator for a firsthand look at the cockpit. The two bantered back and forth easily, Clinton at one point joking that Glenn's medical data would be suspect because "he really hasn't aged in the last 40 years."[37]

Glenn's superior conditioning and excellent health became an issue among those debating the merits of the planned medical tests. Critics argued that he was an atypical test subject, and the medical data his flight would generate could not be adequately compared to anyone else's. In his defense, Glenn noted that the data collected by scientists studying his reactions to the flight would represent the beginning of a process that should continue on future missions. "You've got to start somewhere," he noted. "I'm proud to be that first data point."[38]

The Space Ambassador

As the time finally arrived for the shuttle to lift off, the degree to which America still celebrated John Glenn and all that he represented was abundantly evident. Large crowds, estimated at more than a million, filled the area around the launch site, scouting out the best view. Television and radio covered the launch live, and more than 3,500 journalists crowded into the press area to watch. Walter Cronkite, the CBS News anchor long associated with the space program's best moments, came out of retirement to offer historical perspective on the flight.

Just prior to lift off, the voice of Scott Carpenter could be heard, an emotional echo of the greeting he had offered his fellow Mercury astronaut thirty-six years earlier, at Glenn's first launch: "Good luck, have a safe flight, and once again, Godspeed, John Glenn."

The nine-day mission proceeded flawlessly, its famous payload specialist cheerfully performing the biomedical experiments he'd been assigned, although he wasn't enamored of the frequent blood tests (he jokingly referred to them as "bloodletting").

His most important contribution, however, was the inspiration he provided to young and old alike. Glenn's infectious enthusiasm for spaceflight had not diminished during the three and a half decades he'd waited to fly again in space. Chatting with several groups of children on the third day of the mission via a radio link, he described the value of the shuttle experience:

"It's a benefit to people right there on Earth to do all the things that we're learning. The science has gone from learning just how to do this, how to get into space, to 83 different research experiments that we have onboard on this particular flight."

Asked by one student if being in orbit made him feel any younger, Glenn replied, "I guess I feel young all the time. That's the reason I volunteered to come up here. But it's a great place up here, and I'm having a great time."[39]

When *Discovery* touched down at the end of its nine-day mission, Glenn emerged from the orbiter healthy and happy, showing few effects of his journey into the uncharted territory where space and age intersect. In keeping with the way he'd lived his entire life, he returned to space determined to do well; having accomplished that mission, he came back to earth as space's great ambassador, bringing the heavens a bit closer for all those who ever wondered what was out there, at any point in their lives.

NASA administrator Dan Goldin had accurately predicted the most important impact of the flight shortly before it had launched. "The long lasting impact of this is John Glenn talking about science, especially to young people," he said. "To me, that is the real payoff. I think it's a heightened ability to communicate."[40]

A Legacy of Peace

With the advent of the space shuttle, America's first era of space exploration had come to a close. The shuttle system's utilitarian approach to space has largely precluded the sort of "quantum leap" missions that many of the Mercury, Gemini, and Apollo flights represented in their day.

It is not difficult to calculate the contributions of that first era, however. In a time when hundreds of people can recount their experiences in space and children can realistically look forward to the chance that one day they too will slip free of earth's hold, Alan Shepard's first suborbital catapult ride seems all the more important to everything that has come since.

The U.S. space program of the new millennium owes a great deal to those early days: to the space race that advanced the common cause of space exploration despite the cynical mistrust that sparked and sustained it, and to the hard work of the thousands who spent their days developing a whole new world of equipment and systems, embroidering a path into space and ultimately to the surface of the moon from the whole cloth of unproven theory and romantic dreams.

Above all, the near-routine of today's continual shuttle into the heavens—and whatever the expanding future may hold—is a tribute to the astronauts who led the way, blazing the trail on top of brilliantly lit rockets, blasting into a vast unknown void, testing the most intimate essence within themselves. They proved that the ultimate value of the space program is still the priceless experience of a single human being telling the story of his encounter with strange new places such as Hadley Rille in the mountains of the moon, or relating the warm glow of the good earth as it appears from the faraway vantage point of lunar orbit.

The Mercury, Gemini, and Apollo projects delivered on the long-ago promise of the martyred President Kennedy, and also gave the American people a gauge of the positive force of their own collective will, beyond the circumstances of the day. A spirit that had in the past been most frequently exercised and tested in the agonies of war—for independence, for identity, for freedom—was transformed in the space program into a bright national endeavor of peace, and a legacy to continually be taken up again and again.

Chronology: The First Era in Space, 1957–1975

October 4, 1957   Soviet Union launches *Sputnik 1* satellite on top of an intercontinental ballistic missile (ICBM), inaugurating the space age and causing a public outcry in the United States. Americans fear that space achievement implies Soviet military superiority.

November 3, 1957   Soviet Union launches *Sputnik 2* satellite with a dog, Laika, aboard.

January 31, 1958   United States launches *Explorer 1* satellite. Soviet leader Nikita Khrushchev ridicules the device for being "no larger than a tiny orange."

April 1958   President Dwight Eisenhower proposes new civilian agency to oversee all U.S. space activity that is not specifically military in nature.

May 15, 1958   Soviets launch *Sputnik 3* satellite, a cone-shaped probe designed to conduct scientific tests automatically while in orbit.

October 1, 1958   National Aeronautics and Space Administration (NASA) is formed, with T. Keith Glennan as its first Administrator.

November 1958   Robert Gilruth is placed in charge of a small group of NASA engineers known as the Space Task Group. By the end of the year their work is officially christened Project Mercury.

April 9, 1959   America's first astronauts, the "Mercury Seven," are introduced to the media.

October 7, 1959   Soviets launch *Luna 3* probe, which transmits the first photos of the far side of the moon.

November 8, 1960   Senator John F. Kennedy of Massachusetts defeats Vice President Richard M. Nixon in the 1960 presidential election.

April 12, 1961   Soviets launch *Vostok 1*, with cosmonaut Yuri Gagarin aboard. Gagarin completes one orbit of the earth, becoming the first human being in space, and returns safely.

April 16, 1961   Fourteen hundred Cuban exiles backed by the U.S. government attempt to invade Cuba in the Bay of Pigs debacle. The invasion is quickly routed, and Cuban president Fidel Castro promptly converts his military victory into fodder for anti-American propaganda.

May 5, 1961   Alan Shepard becomes the first American in space, aboard the *Freedom 7* Mercury capsule. His suborbital flight lasts fifteen minutes, twenty-eight seconds, and becomes an inspiration to President Kennedy to increase the nation's commitment to the space program.

May 25, 1961	In a special message to Congress on urgent national needs, President Kennedy sets the goal of landing a man on the moon before the end of the decade.
June 1, 1961	Seven weeks after Yuri Gagarin's historic flight, Soviet leader Nikita Khrushchev warns President Kennedy that the Soviet Union intends to sign a peace treaty with East Germany by the end of the year, effectively isolating West Berlin.
July 21, 1961	Gus Grissom is launched into space in the *Liberty Bell 7* capsule. The mission goes well, but a malfunction of the spacecraft's explosive hatch causes the capsule to sink after splashdown. Grissom barely escapes drowning, but is uninjured.
August 6, 1961	Soviets launch *Vostok 2* with cosmonaut Gherman Titov aboard; he spends a full day in space, making seventeen orbits.
August 13, 1961	Just after midnight, East German troops begin building the Berlin Wall.
August 30, 1961	Disregarding the moratorium on nuclear arms testing that has been in effect for the past three years, the Soviets detonate 100–megaton nuclear weapons in the atmosphere.
February 20, 1962	John Glenn becomes the first American to orbit the earth, aboard the Mercury capsule *Friendship 7*. After nearly five hours in space, Glenn survives a dramatic reentry when a faulty switch erroneously indicates that the heat shield on his capsule is missing or damaged. Following the flight, he is given special honors by President Kennedy in a White House ceremony and mil-

lions cheer his achievement at a ticker tape parade in New York City.

May 24, 1962

Scott Carpenter lifts off aboard the *Aurora 7* capsule in a mission designed to duplicate and validate John Glenn's earlier orbital mission. Carpenter also performs a number of scientific experiments during the flight. A last-minute error leads to a splashdown far from the targeted recovery area, and several tense hours pass before the capsule is located and recovered.

August 11, 1962

Soviets launch *Vostok 3*, followed by *Vostok 4* the following day. The two spacecraft stay close together in orbit for several days before returning to earth.

September 17, 1962

NASA introduces its second group of astronauts to the American public.

October 3, 1962

Wally Schirra is launched into orbit aboard the *Sigma 7* for the longest Mercury mission to date, at a little over nine hours. The flight is virtually flawless, as Schirra carefully conserves fuel and fulfills all of the mission's major objectives.

October 16–29, 1962

President Kennedy and Soviet leader Nikita Khrushchev negotiate a peaceful end to the Cuban missile crisis, and the Soviets agree to remove nuclear weapons from bases they were building in Cuba.

May 15–16, 1963

Gordon Cooper spends America's first day in space, aboard the *Faith 7* Mercury capsule. The first long-endurance flight of the U.S. space program, the flight actually lasts one day, ten hours, nineteen minutes, and forty-nine seconds. A balky electrical system forces the astronaut to take over the spacecraft's controls during reentry, which he does exceptionally well, splashing down safely.

June 14, 1963

Soviets launch *Vostok 5* with cosmonaut Valery Bykovsky aboard, followed by *Vostok 6* two days later with cosmonaut Valentina Tereshkova, the first woman in space. Bykovsky's flight lasts five days, the longest one-man mission.

August 28, 1963

More than 250,000 people gather at the Lincoln Memorial in Washington, D.C., to demand action on civil rights. Dr. Martin Luther King Jr. delivers his powerful "I Have a Dream" speech.

November 22, 1963

President Kennedy is assassinated in Dallas, Texas. While the nation mourns, the Cape Canaveral launch facility is renamed the Kennedy Space Center in his honor.

July 2, 1964

President Lyndon B. Johnson signs the Civil Rights Act of 1964, the most sweeping civil rights law enacted in the twentieth century.

August 2, 1964

North Vietnamese patrol boats attack an American destroyer in the Tonkin Gulf, with a disputed second attack taking place two days later. In response, the U.S. Congress passes the Tonkin Gulf resolution on August 7, giving President Johnson far-reaching power to expand the Vietnam War.

September 27, 1964

The Warren Commission, a seven-member board of inquiry appointed by President Johnson to investigate the assassination of President Kennedy, releases its report to the American public. The commission concludes that Lee Harvey Oswald was the sole assassin, and that

Jack Ruby acted alone when he killed Oswald shortly after the president was murdered.

October 15, 1964   China conducts its first test of nuclear weapons.

October 12, 1964   Soviets launch *Voskhod 1*, with the first-ever three-man crew: Vladimir Komarov, Konstantin Feoktistov, and Boris Yegorov. Soviet leader Nikita Khrushchev calls the crew during the flight; by the time the spacecraft lands after one day in space, Khrushchev has been removed from office. New leaders Leonid Brezhnev and Aleksei Kosygin greets the cosmonauts when they return to earth.

November 3, 1964   President Johnson is reelected in a landslide win over Senator Barry Goldwater of Arizona.

March 7, 1965   Civil rights marchers are violently confronted by police in Selma, Alabama, resulting in serious injuries to more than fifty men and women.

March 18, 1965   Soviets launch *Voskhod 2* with cosmonauts Pavel Belyayev and Alexei Leonov; Leonov achieves the first-ever spacewalk (twelve minutes, nine seconds).

March 23, 1965   The first manned Gemini capsule, *Gemini 3*, is launched with Gus Grissom and John Young as its crew. The new spacecraft performs admirably well, making three orbits before splashing down a little less than five hours after launch.

June 3–7, 1965   James McDivitt and Ed White travel into space aboard *Gemini 4*. White achieves the first American spacewalk, a twenty-two-minute-EVA (extravehicular activity) on the first day of the mission.

August 21–29, 1965   Aboard *Gemini 5*, Gordon Cooper and Pete Conrad simulate rendezvous procedures and spend eight days in space.

December 1965   The number of U.S. troops in Vietnam passes 200,000.

December 4–18, 1965   Aboard *Gemini 7*, Frank Borman and Jim Lovell set a new standard for long-duration spaceflight, at fourteen days.

December 15–16, 1965   Wally Schirra and Tom Stafford achieve the first space rendezvous, maneuvering their *Gemini 6* capsule into close proximity with *Gemini 7*.

January 14, 1966   Sergei Korolev, the chief designer of the Soviet space program and the key impetus behind most of its early achievements, dies after an operation. Vasily Mishin is appointed as the program's new director, and he immediately begins work on the Soyuz and L-1 spacecraft designed to put a cosmonaut on the moon.

March 16, 1966   Neil Armstrong and David Scott are launched aboard *Gemini 8*. They achieve the first docking of two vehicles in space, when they link their capsule to an unmanned Agena rocket target vehicle. Their spacecraft then begins spinning out of control, forcing the mission to be cut short. Following NASA's emergency procedures, they return immediately to earth, splashing down safely a little less than eleven hours after launch.

June 3–6, 1966   The *Gemini 9* crew of Tom Stafford and Eugene Cernan practice rendezvous procedures, and Cernan makes a difficult two-hour spacewalk. They are unable to achieve their docking objective, however, because of a malfunction in their target vehicle.

July 18–21, 1966   John Young and Michael Collins practice rendezvous procedures aboard *Gemini 10*, and Collins makes two spacewalks totaling eighty-eight minutes.

September 12–15, 1966 During the *Gemini 11* mission, Pete Conrad and Richard Gordon achieve rendezvous and docking and tethered flight, with their Gemini capsule tied to an unmanned target vehicle. Gordon also makes three spacewalks during the mission, and on their return to earth, they achieve the first completely automatic reentry of the U.S. program—an important procedure to master for the coming Apollo program.

November 11–15, 1966 The final mission of the Gemini program, *Gemini 12*, is manned by Jim Lovell and Buzz Aldrin. They achieve rendezvous, docking, and station keeping, and Aldrin compiles a record spacewalk total of five hours while trying out a number of new procedures that will make EVAs easier and more productive.

December 1966   The number of U.S. troops in Vietnam passes 400,000.

January 27, 1967   *Apollo 1* fire. Astronauts Gus Grissom, Ed White, and Roger Chaffee are killed during a test of the Apollo spacecraft.

April 23, 1967   Soviets launch *Soyuz 1* in hopes of achieving rendezvous and docking with *Soyuz 2*, to be launched later. *Soyuz 1* suffers a major systems failure and is forced to return to earth early; on landing, its parachute lines twist, causing it to crash to earth violently, killing cosmonaut Vladimir Komarov upon impact.

November 9, 1967   *Apollo 4* is launched; the unmanned mission is the first since the *Apollo 1* fire, and the first live test of a Saturn V rocket, which performs well.

January 30, 1968
In Vietnam, the North Vietnamese and Viet Cong launch a major attack on the first day of the Vietnamese new year. The Tet offensive is the decisive turning point in the war, as the Communists prove their ability to strike at the heart of American and South Vietnamese defenses. As the crisis unfolds, public opinion polls show for the first time that a majority of the American public no longer supports the war.

January 31, 1968
President Johnson announces that he will not seek reelection.

March 16, 1968
Senator Robert F. Kennedy of New York announces his candidacy for the presidency.

March 27, 1968
Yuri Gagarin, the first human in space, is killed in a MiG 15 airplane crash during a training flight.

April 4, 1968
American civil rights leader Dr. Martin Luther King is assassinated in Memphis, Tennessee. Mourning is mixed with sporadic violence, as rioting breaks out in large cities across the United States.

June 6, 1968
While campaigning for the presidency in Los Angeles, Robert Kennedy is assassinated shortly after winning the California Democratic primary.

August 1968
Violent clashes between police and antiwar demonstrators at the Democratic National Convention in Chicago, Illinois are televised live throughout the nation.

August 21, 1968   The Soviet Union invades Czechoslovakia.

October 11–22, 1968   Mercury veteran Wally Schirra flies his last mis-
                         sion for NASA aboard *Apollo 7* before retiring.
                         He is joined by rookie astronauts Donn Eisele
                         and Walter Cunningham for 163 orbits around
                         the earth, in a flight that validates the many
                         changes made to the Apollo spacecraft since the
                         Apollo 1 fire.

November 5, 1968   Richard Nixon defeats Vice President Hubert
                         Humphrey in the U.S. presidential election.

December 1968   The number of American troops in Vietnam
                         reaches its high of 540,000.

December 21–27, 1968   Frank Borman, Jim Lovell, and William
                         Anders become the first human beings to or-
                         bit the moon, as *Apollo 8*, the "Christmas
                         Apollo," successfully enters into lunar orbit.
                         The astronauts read from the Book of Genesis
                         on Christmas Eve, captivating a worldwide
                         audience on earth.

January 14, 1969   Soviets launch *Soyuz 4*, followed by *Soyuz 5* the
                         next day. The two spacecraft achieve docking and
                         crew transfers, prompting Soviet leadership to
                         hail the joint flight as the "first experimental space
                         station." It is the same mission that was planned
                         for *Soyuz 1* and *Soyuz 2* in April 1967, when
                         Vladimir Komarov was killed.

February 21, 1969   Soviets attempt first launch of N-1 rocket, the
                         equivalent to the American Saturn V that proved
                         crucial to the Apollo program. Launch fails after
                         seventy seconds, resulting in fire and explosion.

March 3–13, 1969   Aboard *Apollo 9*, James McDivitt, David Scott,
                         and Russell Schweickart test out the Apollo lu-

nar module, performing all maneuvers necessary for the eventual landing on the moon.

May 18–26, 1969   *Apollo 10* launch orbits the moon and simu-
lates a lunar landing. Tom Stafford, John Young,
and Eugene Cernan are the crew for this final
test run before the first lunar landing.

July 3, 1969   For the second time in six months, the Soviets
attempt to launch the N-1 rocket that is vital to
their plans for a lunar landing; the rocket ex-
plodes on the launch pad.

July 13, 1969   Soviets launch unmanned *Luna 15* moon probe;
it crashes on the moon on July 21, after
Armstrong and Aldrin walk on the moon but
before they leave. The probe is apparently a
sample-return probe designed to upstage the
manned American effort.

July 16–24, 1969   Neil Armstrong, Buzz Aldrin, and Michael
Collins fly to the moon and back aboard *Apollo
11*. On July 20, Armstrong and Aldrin land
the lunar module *Eagle* and become the first
human beings to walk on the surface of the
moon. During their brief stay, they plant the
American flag, take photographs, gather moon
rocks and core samples, and activate a battery
of scientific instruments while a fascinated
worldwide audience on earth watches them live
on television.

August 15–18, 1969   An estimated half million young people gather
in upstate New York for the Woodstock Music
and Arts Festival.

October 1969   Soviet Union announces that it no longer has
any plans for manned flights to the moon. Development, testing, and test flights related to
manned landings continue through 1973.

November 14–24, 1969 Pete Conrad, Richard Gordon, and Alan Bean journey into space aboard *Apollo 12.* After a shaky launch in which lightning strikes the pad, causing an electrical failure onboard the capsule during the first few minutes of the mission, the flight proceeds more smoothly, and Conrad and Bean land on the moon on November 18. They walk on the lunar surface twice during their stay, and locate and remove parts of the *Surveyor 3* unmanned probe that had landed on the moon years earlier. Gordon, meanwhile, conducts photographic experiments while passing over them in lunar orbit.

November 15, 1969 A massive demonstration against the Vietnam War attracts 250,000 antiwar protesters to Washington, D.C.

November 16, 1969 The American public first becomes aware of the My Lai massacre, in which American soldiers on a search-and-destroy mission decimated the inhabitants of a Vietnamese village. Knowledge of the incident furthers the resolve of those who are openly opposed to the Vietnam War.

April 11–17, 1970 *Apollo 13,* with Jim Lovell, Fred Haise, and Jack Swigert onboard, suffers an explosion during its flight to the moon. With the planned lunar landing out of the question, the crew uses the lunar module as a "lifeboat" instead, employing it to sustain them in place of their severely damaged command and service modules. Perseverance, ingenuity, and uncommon courage on the part of the crew and ground controllers avert a tragedy, and the astronauts splash down safely after six extraordinary days in space.

May 4, 1970 Four students at Kent State University in Kent,

Ohio are killed during a violent confrontation between antiwar protesters and National Guard troops. In protest, more than 125 colleges across the nation are closed over the next few days, and one week later a massive rally takes place outside the White House.

December 1970   The number of American troops in Vietnam is down to 280,000 by year's end.

January 31– / February 9, 1971   America's first space hero, Alan Shepard, returns to the heavens aboard *Apollo 14*, with fellow crew members Stuart Roosa and Ed Mitchell. Shepard and Mitchell land on the moon on February 3 and make two EVAs, aided by a hand-pulled cart. They make an arduous climb amid the hills of the moon's Fra Mauro region, collecting interesting rock samples, and before they leave, Shepard entertains his audience on earth by hitting several golf balls in an ad hoc demonstration of the moon's reduced gravitational pull.

June 13, 1971   The *New York Times* begins publishing the Pentagon Papers, the Defense Department's classified history of U.S. involvement in the Vietnam War. Two days later the Justice Department obtains a temporary restraining order, beginning a legal battle that is eventually resolved in the newspaper's favor.

July 26–August 7, 1971 David Scott, Alfred Worden, and James Irwin travel to the moon aboard *Apollo 15*; Scott and Irwin land in the Hadley Rille valley, next to the moon's Apennine Mountains, on July 30. They make good use of the lunar rover, available on this trip for the first time, to conduct far-ranging EVAs, and discover an ancient lunar sample that scientists later call the "Genesis rock" for the clues it provides about how the moon and the earth were formed.

December 1971

The number of American troops in Vietnam is down to 140,000 by end of the year.

February 21–27, 1972

President Nixon visits China.

April 16–27, 1972

John Young, Thomas Mattingly, and Charles Duke take their turn at the moon during the *Apollo 16* mission. Young and Duke land on the lunar surface on April 20 and make three EVAs, spending a total of more than twenty hours outside their lunar module and gathering more than 200 pounds of moon rocks.

May 8, 1972

Vowing to stop the flow of arms and other military supplies until the enemy agrees to mediate an end to the Vietnam War, President Nixon orders the mining of all North Vietnamese ports.

May 15, 1972

Alabama Governor George C. Wallace is critically wounded in an assassination attempt as he campaigns for the presidency in Laurel, Maryland. He recovers but is partially paralyzed for the rest of his life.

May 22–29, 1972

President Nixon visits the Soviet Union and meets with Soviet leader Leonid Brezhnev at a historic summit meeting in Moscow. The two leaders sign the SALT I treaty on May 26.

June 17, 1972

Five men are arrested for breaking into the Democratic Party national headquarters at the Watergate complex in Washington, D.C.

September 5, 1972

Eleven members of Israel's Olympic team are killed by Arab terrorists during a twenty-three-hour hostage ordeal at the 1972 Olympics in Munich, West Germany.

November 7, 1972   President Nixon is reelected in a landslide win over Senator George McGovern of South Dakota.

December 7–19, 1972   Eugene Cernan, Ronald Evans, and Harrison Schmitt travel to the moon during *Apollo 17*, the last mission in the Apollo series. Schmitt, a geologist, becomes the first professional scientist to walk on the moon after he and Cernan land on December 11. They make three EVAs and spend a total of more than twenty-two hours on the lunar surface.

January 27, 1973   U.S. Secretary of State William P. Rogers signs peace accord in Paris, France, that officially ends American involvement in the Vietnam War.

March 29, 1973   The last American troops leave Vietnam.

April 30, 1973   Several high-ranking aides to President Nixon resign amid charges of obstruction of justice in the Watergate scandal.

May 14, 1973   *Skylab* is launched. The first crew is scheduled to follow the next day, but damage to the lab during launch causes their flight to be delayed while NASA engineers work through procedures for repairs. The space station remains in orbit until July of 1979, when it breaks apart during reentry into earth's atmosphere, scattering its surviving pieces over largely uninhabited portions of Australia.

May 25–
June 22, 1973   During the *Skylab 2* mission, Pete Conrad, Paul Weitz, and Joseph Kerwin make repairs to the damaged station and conduct medical and other experiments.

July 28– September 25, 1973	The *Skylab 3* crew of Alan Bean, Jack Lousma, and Owen Garriott spend several productive months aboard the space station, working long hours to conduct experiments and make further repairs.
October 10, 1973	After pleading no contest to charges of income tax evasion, Spiro T. Agnew becomes the first vice president in U.S. history to resign from office.
October 12, 1973	President Nixon nominates Gerald R. Ford, minority leader of the House of Representatives, to replace Spiro Agnew as vice president. On the same day, the U.S. Court of Appeals rules that President Nixon must relinquish to the federal district court tape recordings that may contain evidence implicating him in crimes related to the Watergate burglary and coverup.
November 16, 1973	The *Skylab 4* mission is launched, with crew members Gerald Carr, William Pogue, and Edward Gibson. The final—and most ambitious—trip to *Skylab* produces interesting scientific results, as the crew observes and photographs Comet Kohoutek and the complete cycle of a solar flare. The crew makes 1,214 orbits and sets a new record for the longest American stay in space before splashing down on February 8, 1974.
May 9, 1974	Judiciary Committee of the U.S. House of Representatives begins hearings to consider the impeachment of President Nixon.
August 9, 1974	President Nixon becomes the first president in U.S. history to resign from office.

September 8, 1974   President Ford pardons former president Nixon for any crimes he may have committed while in office.

April 5, 1975   Cosmonauts Vasili Lazarev and Oleg Makarov survive the first human launch abort when their rocket fails and they are jettisoned some nine hundred miles from the launch pad.

April 30, 1975   The South Vietnamese capital of Saigon falls to the Communist Viet Cong, ending the Vietnam War. The evacuation of the last remaining Americans from the U.S. embassy in Saigon is completed just hours before the city is overrun.

July 15, 1975   For the first time, the United States and USSR cooperate on a space venture, when the Apollo-Soyuz Test Project (ASTP) is launched. Once in space, the Apollo crew of Tom Stafford, Vance Brand, and Mercury veteran Deke Slayton meet up with Soviet *Soyuz 19* cosmonauts Alexei Leonov and Valeri Kubasov on July 17. The two spacecraft dock and crew members visit in each others' quarters, receiving messages from American president Gerald Ford and Soviet leader Leonid Brezhnev. The Soviet crew returns to earth on July 21, and the last Apollo splashes down in the Pacific Ocean on July 24.

Notes

Chapter 1. NASA Lifts Off: The 1950s

1. Pach and Richardson, *Presidency*, p. 171.
2. Arnold, *Man in Space*, pp. 12–18.
3. Oberg, *Red Star*, p. 63.
4. Newhouse, *War and Peace*, pp. 117–118.
5. Newhouse, *War and Peace*, p. 119.
6. Oberg, *Red Star*, pp. 33–34.
7. Leopold, "Navy Spy Satellite," p. 22.
8. Pach and Richardson, *Presidency*, p. 171.
9. Leopold, "Navy Spy Satellite,"p. 1.
10. Arnold, *Man in Space*, p. 19.
11. Arnold, *Man in Space*, p. 22.
12. Arnold, *Man in Space*, pp. 20–21.
13. Pach and Richardson, *Presidency*, pp. 179–180.
14. Arnold, *Man in Space*, pp. 40, 42.
15. Oberg, *Red Star*, p. 118.
16. Arnold, *Man in Space*, p. 34.
17. Oberg, *Red Star*, p. 77.
18. Arnold, *Man in Space*, pp. 20–21.
19. Arnold, *Man in Space*, pp. 21–24.
20. Chafe, *Unfinished Journey*, p. 114.
21. Newhouse, *War and Peace*, pp. 117–119.

Chapter 2. Project Mercury: Setting the Sights

1. Sorenson, *Kennedy*, pp. 523–529.
2. Kennedy, *Tide*, p. 39.
3. Oberg, *Red Star*, p. 63.

4. Arnold, *Man in Space*, pp. 28–29.
5. Oberg, *Red Star*, pp. 52–53.
6. Arnold, *Man in Space*, p. 123
7. Oberg, *Red Star*, pp. 54–55.
8. Oberg, *Red Star*, p. 63.
9. Swenson et al., *New Ocean*, p. 111.
10. Arnold, *Man in Space*, p. 43.
11. Hurt, *Mankind*, p. 94.
12. Slayton, "Everybody," pp. 75–81.
13. Williams et al., *Mercury Summary.*
14. Swenson et al., *New Ocean*, pp. 172–178.
15. The astronauts' attitude, outlook, and personal experiences are available from a wide array of sources. The earliest account in book form seems to be *We Seven*, a collection of essays about various aspects of the Mercury program, which they collectively authored and published in 1962.
16. Shepard, "First American," pp. 173–199.
17. Oberg, *Red Star*, p. 84.
18. Swenson et al., *New Ocean*, pp. 360–361.
19. Swenson et al., *New Ocean*, pp. 354–356.
20. Shepard and Slayton, *Moon Shot*, pp. 131–132.
21. Sorenson, *Kennedy*, p. 525.
22. Kennedy, *Tide*, p. 88.
23. Sorenson, *Kennedy*, p. 525.
24. Sorenson, *Kennedy*, p. 524.
25. Swenson et al., *New Ocean*, pp. 377–378.
26. Swenson et al., *New Ocean*, pp. 366–367.
27. Grissom, "Liberty Bell," pp. 205–228. Thanks to the enormous advances in the technology of deep-sea exploration, the *Liberty Bell* capsule was located on the floor of the Atlantic Ocean early in 1999. Video of the tiny craft offered silent testimony to the engineering and manufacturing expertise of the space program's early years; even after more than three decades, *Liberty Bell* appeared remarkably well preserved.
28. Arnold, *Man in Space*, pp. 44–45.
29. Newhouse, *War and Peace*, pp. 155–157.
30. Shepard and Slayton, *Moon Shot*, p. 144.
31. Carpenter, "Confirmation," pp. 337–346.
32. Glenn, "Mission," pp. 303–304.
33. Glenn, "Mission," pp. 381–387.
34. Shepard and Slayton, *Moon Shot*, p. 152.
35. NASA, "Mercury."
36. Shepard and Slayton, *Moon Shot*, pp. 156–157.
37. Carpenter, "Confirmation," pp. 337–346.
38. The group two astronauts figured heavily in the Apollo program. Of the nine members of the group, seven flew Apollo missions, and three (Armstrong, Conrad, and Young) landed on the moon. Elliot See and group three astronaut Charles Bassett were killed in an airplane crash in 1966, just three months before they would have flown in space on *Gemini 9*, and Ed White was killed in the *Apollo 1* fire in 1967.

39. Arnold, *Man in Space*, p. 46.
40. Swenson et al., *New Ocean*, pp. 494–503.
41. Oberg, *Red Star*, pp. 67–69.
42. Swenson et al., *New Ocean*, p. 506.
43. Oberg, *Red Star*, p. 69.
44. Dunn, "Pioneering Pilot," p. 3B.
45. Group three's fourteen astronauts included ten who flew Apollo missions and four (Aldrin, Bean, Cernan, and Scott) who walked on the moon. Thus groups two and three produced nineteen of the thirty-three astronauts who participated in Apollo (including Ed White and Roger Chaffee, who died in the *Apollo 1* fire) and seven of the twelve who walked on the moon.
46. Swenson et al., *New Ocean*, p. 508.

Chapter 3. Project Gemini: A Bridge to the Moon

1. Oberg, *Red Star*, p. 84.
2. Arnold, *Man in Space*, p. 32.
3. Arnold, *Man in Space*, p. 34.
4. Johnson, *Vantage Point*, pp. 281–285.
5. Shepard and Slayton, *Moon Shot*, p. 165.
6. Arnold, *Man in Space*, p. 33.
7. Oberg, *Red Star*, pp. 79–83.
8. Oberg, *Red Star*, 79–86.
9. NASA, "Gemini."
10. Hacker and Alexander, *Titans*, p. 56.
11. NASA, "Gemini."
12. Aldrin, *Return to Earth*, p. 183.
13. Hacker and Alexander, *Titans*, pp. 203–209.
14. Shepard and Slayton, *Moon Shot*, p. 170.
15. Arnold, *Man in Space*, p. 51.
16. NASA, "Gemini."
17. Shepard and Slayton, *Moon Shot*, pp. 179–180.
18. Shepard and Slayton, *Moon Shot*, pp. 181–182
19. Arnold, *Man in Space*, p. 51.
20. NASA, "Gemini."
21. Arnold, *Man in Space*, p. 52.
22. Hacker and Alexander, *Titans*, pp. 285–291.
23. Arnold, *Man in Space*, p. 37.
24. Aldrin, *Return to Earth*, pp. 163–166.
25. Cernan, "Price," p. 6.
26. NASA, "Gemini."
27. Shepard and Slayton, *Moon Shot*, pp. 183–185.
28. Shepard and Slayton, *Moon Shot*, p. 186.
29. Arnold, *Man in Space*, p. 54.
30. Hacker and Alexander, *Titans*, pp. 337–339.
31. Hacker and Alexander, *Titans*, pp. 344–351.

32. Hacker and Alexander, *Titans*, p. 356.
33. Hacker and Alexander, *Titans*, pp. 360–370.
34. Aldrin, *Return to Earth*, pp. 173–174
35. Aldrin, *Return to Earth*, pp. 174–175.
36. Aldrin, *Return to Earth*, pp. 181–183.

Chapter 4. *Apollo 1:* Lives in Eclipse

1. Arnold, *Man in Space*, pp. 62–63.
2. Murray and Cox, *Apollo*, p. 186.
3. Hurt, *Mankind*, p. 80.
4. Zornio, "Detailed Biographies." For a full-length biography of Roger Chaffee, see *On Course to the Stars: The Roger B. Chaffee Story*, by C. Donald Chrysler (Grand Rapids: Kregal, 1968).
5. Zornio, "Detailed Biographies."
6. Zornio, "Detailed Biographies." For full-length treatments of Gus Grissom, see the posthumously published autobiography *Gemini: A Personal Account of Man's Venture into Space* (New York: Macmillan, 1968), and the biography *Starfall*, by Betty Grissom and Henry Still (New York: Thomas V. Crowell, 1974).
7. Murray and Cox, *Apollo*, pp. 221–222.
8. Arnold, *Man in Space*, p. 64.
9. Shepard and Slayton, *Moon Shot*, pp. 192–193.
10. Shepard and Slayton, *Moon Shot*, p. 195.
11. Shepard and Slayton, *Moon Shot*, pp. 196–197.
12. Shepard and Slayton, *Moon Shot*, p. 198.
13. Oberg, *Red Star*, pp. 90–96.
14. Arnold, *Man in Space*, pp. 35–37.
15. Murray and Cox, *Apollo*, pp. 203–205.
16. Arnold, *Man in Space*, p. 64.
17. Arnold, *Man in Space*, p. 64.
18. Hurt, *Mankind*, p. 83.
19. Murray and Cox, *Apollo*, pp. 309–314.

Chapter 5. Apollo Before the Moon: Into the Light

1. Arnold, *Man in Space*, p. 69.
2. Murray and Cox, *Apollo*, p. 341.
3. Hurt, *Mankind*, pp. 94–95.
4. Shepard and Slayton, *Moon Shot*, pp. 195–196, 222.
5. Shepard and Slayton, *Moon Shot*, pp. 221–222.
6. Murray and Cox, *Apollo*, p. 324.
7. Shepard and Slayton, *Moon Shot*, pp. 228–229.
8. Shepard and Slayton, *Moon Shot*, p. 225.
9. Shepard and Slayton, *Moon Shot*, p. 233.
10. Murray and Cox, *Apollo*, p. 333.
11. Arnold, *Man in Space*, p. 37.
12. Nixon, *RN*, vol. 1, p. 530.

13. Arnold, *Man in Space*, pp. 35–37.
14. Arnold, *Man in Space*, p. 73.
15. Shepard and Slayton, *Moon Shot*, p. 242.
16. Jones, "Apollo Journal."

Chapter 6. *Apollo 11:* Life on an Ancient World

1. On its way to the moon, *Apollo 11* lifted off on July 16, 1969—coincidentally the twenty-fourth anniversary of the first live test of an atomic bomb, at Alamogordo, New Mexico, in 1945.
2. Shepard and Slayton, *Moon Shot*, pp. 247–248.
3. Armstrong, Collins, and Aldrin, *First on the Moon*, p. 403. Like the Mercury astronauts, the crew of *Apollo 11* wrote a joint memoir following their mission.
4. Aldrin, *Return to Earth*, pp. 220–221.
5. On the day following the landing, the *New York Times* estimated the television audience for Armstrong's first step to be "hundreds of millions."
6. Jones, "Apollo Journal." Although the particulars of the *Apollo 11* landing have been recorded in many books, magazines, and newspapers, I have relied primarily on Eric Jones's "Apollo Lunar Surface Journal" for exact quotations and technical details. Available on the World Wide Web at NASA's History Office Web site (see bibliography for address), the Apollo "Journal" is authoritative in its completeness and its accuracy. It includes the entire, corrected transcripts of all audio and video transmissions for each lunar landing mission and provides commentary and context via excerpts from the technical debriefings that followed each flight and subsequent interviews with ten of the involved astronauts.
7. Aldrin, *Return to Earth*, p. 230.
8. Jones, "Apollo Journal."
9. Aldrin, *Return to Earth*, p. 233.
10. Aldrin, *Return to Earth*, p. 236.
11. Jones, "Apollo Journal."
12. Shepard and Slayton, *Moon Shot*, pp. 248–249.
13. *NASA 25 Years.*
14. Aldrin, *Return to Earth*, p. 229.
15. *NASA 25 Years.*
16. *NASA 25 Years.*
17. *NASA 25 Years.*
18. Nixon, *RN* vol. 1, p. 532.

Chapter 7. *Apollo 12* and *Apollo 13:* Storms in Space

1. Wolfert, "Year of the Moon," p. 59.
2. Shepard and Slayton, *Moon Shot*, pp. 255–256.
3. Hurt, *Mankind*, pp. 170–171.
4. *NASA 25 Years.*
5. Arnold, *Man in Space*, pp. 85–86.
6. Murray and Cox, *Apollo*, p. 449.

7. Lovell and Kluger, *Apollo 13*, pp. 88–90.
8. Jones, "Apollo Journal."
9. Lovell and Kluger, *Apollo 13*, p. 103.
10. Lovell and Kluger, *Apollo 13*, p. 104.
11. Lovell and Kluger, *Apollo 13*, p. 110.
12. Lovell and Kluger, *Apollo 13*, p. 113.
13. Lovell and Kluger, *Apollo 13*, pp. 270–271.
14. Lovell and Kluger, *Apollo 13*, pp. 305–308.
15. Jones, "Apollo Journal."
16. Lovell and Kluger, *Apollo 13*, p. 351.
17. Lovell and Kluger, *Apollo 13*, p. 367.
18. Jones, "Apollo Journal."

Chapter 8. Before the Short Day Ends: Apollo in Twilight

1. Murray and Cox, *Apollo*, p. 449.
2. Hurt, *Mankind*, pp. 219–222.
3. Shepard and Slayton, *Moon Shot*, pp. 290–291.
4. Hurt, *Mankind*, p. 222.
5. Hurt, *Mankind*, pp. 223–224.
6. Jones, "Apollo Journal."
7. Jones, "Apollo Journal."
8. *NASA 25 Years.*
9. NASA, "Apollo."
10. Jones, "Apollo Journal."
11. Shepard and Slayton, *Moon Shot*, pp. 314–317.
12. Shepard and Slayton, *Moon Shot*, pp. 317–318.
13. Arnold, *Man in Space*, pp. 38–39.
14. Based on transcripts of audiotapes he made during his retirement, the book *Khrushchev Remembers: The Glasnost Tapes* (translated and edited by Jerrold L. Schecter with Vyacheslav V. Luchkov [Boston: Little, Brown, 1990]) clearly demonstrates the former Soviet leader's preference for a manned landing on the moon, rather than having to settle for unmanned probes, robotic vehicles, and sample-return missions. Finally released in the West some twenty years after the publication of his memoirs, the book quotes Khrushchev, circa 1970: "The American astronauts have already reached the moon. Now our radio, press, and television all say that we are ahead, but the evidence of this is not serious . . . it was important for man to get to the moon, rather than an unmanned system, no matter how independent or smart it might be. Such a system is a creation of man, and so when man himself—the creator of an unmanned system— visits the moon and looks all around for himself, he understands better and more deeply than would have been possible with technological means."
15. Arnold, *Man in Space*, pp. 101–102.
16. Murray and Cox, *Apollo*, pp. 449–450.
17. *NASA 25 Years.*
18. *NASA 25 Years.*
19. Jones, "Apollo Journal."

20. Cernan, "Price," p. 7.
21. *NASA 25 Years.*
22. Arnold, *Man in Space*, p. 78.
23. NASA, "Apollo."
24. *NASA 25 Years.*
25. Hurt, *Mankind*, p. 245.
26. NASA, "Apollo."
27. Jones, "Apollo Journal."
28. *NASA 25 Years.*
29. NASA, "Apollo."
30. Jones, "Apollo Journal."
31. *NASA 25 Years.*
32. Hurt, *Mankind*, p. 251.
33. Jones, "Apollo Journal."
34. Jones, "Apollo Journal."

Chapter 9. *Skylab*: A Place in Space

1. Shepard and Slayton, *Moon Shot*, pp. 332–333.
2. *NASA 25 Years.*
3. NASA, "Apollo."
4. NASA, "Apollo."
5. Arnold, *Man in Space*, p. 119.
6. Shepard and Slayton, *Moon Shot*, p. 333.

Chapter 10. Apollo-Soyuz Test Project: A Handshake Across the Heavens

1. *NASA 25 Years.*
2. Shepard and Slayton, *Moon Shot*, pp. 326–327.
3. Ezell and Ezell, *Partnership*, pp. 170–173.
4. Ezell and Ezell, *Partnership*, pp. 185–187.
5. Shepard and Slayton, *Moon Shot*, pp. 340–341.
6. Arnold, *Man in Space*, p. 125.
7. Oberg, *Red Star*, pp. 56, 158.
8. Ezell and Ezell, *Partnership*, pp. 318–320.
9. *NASA 25 Years.*
10. Shepard and Slayton, *Moon Shot*, p. 355.
11. Shepard and Slayton, *Moon Shot*, pp. 355–356.
12. Ezell and Ezell, *Partnership*, pp. 328–330.
13. Ezell and Ezell, *Partnership*, pp. 340–341.
14. *NASA 25 Years.*
15. Oberg, *Red Star*, p. 139.
16. Ezell and Ezell, *Partnership*, pp. 347–349.
17. Ezell and Ezell, *Partnership*, p. 349.
18. Nixon, *RN*, vol. 2, pp. 99–100.

19. In his memoir *A Time to Heal* (New York: Harper and Row, 1979), Ford alludes briefly to the Apollo-Soyuz Test Project as part of Nixon's "grand strategy to move from the Cold War to a policy of detente with the Soviets." He does not mention the mission by name, however; he refers to it only as "the joint space effort" (128).

Chapter 11. The 1970s: Journeys Without and Within

1. Chafe, *Unfinished Journey*, p. 399.
2. Wicker, *One of Us*.
3. Chafe, *Unfinished Journey*, pp. 450–454.

Chapter 12. Echoes: The Shuttle Era and Beyond

1. *Life*, "Bird." The first shuttle ever built, *Enterprise* was actually a test vehicle designed only for trying out the program's concept, equipment, and systems in earth's atmosphere. It was never intended to fly in space.
2. Oberg, *Red Star*, pp. 137–138.
3. Oberg, *Red Star*, pp. 134–136.
4. Wicker, *One of Us*, p. 540.
5. *Peekskill Star*, "NASA Dumping," p. 6B.
6. *New York Times*, "Voyage," p. C3.
7. Powers, *Shuttle*, pp. 60–66.
8. *New York Times*, "Voyage," p. C3.
9. *New York Times*, "Voyage," p. C3.
10. Powers, *Shuttle*, p. 63.
11. *Daily Press*, "Mission," p. 8.
12. Hurt, *Mankind*, p. 298.
13. NASA, *Shuttle Chronology*, p. 1.
14. Collins, "Foreword," p. 12.
15. NASA, *Shuttle Chronology*, p. 2.
16. NASA, *Shuttle Chronology*, p. 2.
17. Powers, *Shuttle*, pp. 134–135.
18. Golden, "Mission Accomplished," pp. 25–26.
19. NASA, *Shuttle Chronology*, pp. 3–4.
20. Golden, "Orbiting," p. 62.
21. Golden, "Tinkering," p. 106.
22. NASA, *Shuttle Chronology*, p. 5.
23. Wilford, "Ground Up," p. 1E.
24. Schieffer and Gates, *Acting President*, p. 278.
25. Lemonick, "Three Minutes," p. 55.
26. Arnold, *Man in Space*, p. 150.
27. Arnold, *Man in Space*, p. 152.
28. Slagle, "Russian Roulette," p. 5.
29. Slagle, "Prober Blasts Off," p. 3.
30. Reagan, *Speaking*, p. 292.

31. *New York Times*, "Tentative Plan," p. C3.
32. NASA, *Shuttle Chronology*.
33. NASA, *Shuttle Chronology*, p. 25.
34. NASA, "Lunar Prospector."
35. Goodman, "Americans Turn High-tech," p. 15A.
36. Lyttle, "American Story," pp. 32–34.
37. Riskind, "Clinton's Visit," p. 3A.
38. Kiernan, "Scientists Plan," p. 21A.
39. Borenstein, "For Children," p. 9A.
40. Borenstein, "For Children," p. 9A.

Bibliography

Aldrin, Edwin E. "Buzz" Jr. with Wayne Warga. *Return To Earth*. New York: Random House, 1973.

Armstrong, Neil, Michael Collins, and Edwin E. Aldrin Jr. with Gene Farmer and Dora Jane Hamblin. *First on the Moon*. Boston: Little, Brown, 1970.

Arnold, H.J.P., ed. *Man in Space: An Illustrated History of Space Flight*. New York: Smithmark, 1993.

Borenstein, Seth. "For Children, Glenn Is 'Just an All Around Hero.'" *The Journal News* (White Plains, New York), November 1, 1998, p. 9A.

Carpenter, Malcolm Scott. "The Confirmation." In M. Scott Carpenter et al., *We Seven*, pp. 329–346. New York: Simon and Schuster, 1962.

Cernan, Eugene. "The Price of Being a Space Hero." *TV Guide*, April 13, 1985, pp. 4–7.

Chafe, William H. *The Unfinished Journey: America Since World War II*. 2d ed. New York: Oxford University Press, 1991.

Collins, Michael. Foreword. In Robert M. Powers, *The World's First Spaceship: Shuttle*. New York: Warner Books, 1980.

Daily Press (Hampton, Virginia). "Mission Heralds Program with Many Applications." April 15, 1981, pp. 1–8.

Dunn, Marcia. "Pioneering Pilot Wants the Chance NASA Promised Her Decades Ago: 'I Would Give My Life to Fly in Space.'" *Peekskill Star*, July 12, 1998, p. 3B.

Ezell, Edward Clinton, and Linda Neuman Ezell. *The Partnership: A History of the Apollo-Soyuz Test Project*. NASA Special Publication SP-4209 (http://www.hq.nasa.gov/office/pao/History/SP-4209/cover.htm). Washington, DC: NASA, 1978.

Glenn Jr., John H. "The Mission." In M. Scott Carpenter et al., *We Seven*, pp. 281–327. New York: Simon and Schuster, 1962.

Golden, Frederic. "Mission Accomplished: Sally Ride and Friends Have the Time of Their Lives." *Time*, July 4, 1983, pp. 22–26.

⸺. "Orbiting with Flash and Buck: A Historic Touchdown Ends Challenger's Bittersweet Journey." *Time*, February 20, 1984, pp. 62–64.

⸺. "Tinkering with Solar Max: Challenger's Astronauts Will Attempt the First Satellite Repair." *Time*, April 9, 1984, p. 106.

Goodman, Ellen. "Americans Turn High-tech Space Traveler into a Mascot." *Peekskill Star*, July 10, 1997, p. 15A.

Grissom, Virgil I. "The Trouble With Liberty Bell." In M. Scott Carpenter et al., *We Seven*, pp. 205–228. New York: Simon and Schuster, 1962.

Hacker, Barton C., and Charles C. Alexander. *On the Shoulders of Titans: A History of Project Gemini.* NASA Special Publication SP-4203 (http://www.hq.nasa.gov/office/pao/History/SP-4203/cover.htm). Washington, DC: NASA, 1977.

Hurt, Harry III. *For All Mankind.* New York: Atlantic Monthly Press, 1988.

Johnson, Lyndon Baines. *The Vantage Point: Perspectives on the Presidency, 1963–1969.* New York: Holt, Rinehart, and Winston, 1971.

Jones, Eric M. *The Apollo Lunar Surface Journal.* Online (http://www.hq.nasa.gov/office/pao/History/alsj/frame.html). Washington, DC: NASA, 1995.

Kennedy, John F. *To Turn the Tide.* John W. Gardner, ed. New York: Popular Library, 1962.

Kiernan, Vincent. "Scientists Plan Varied Experiments for Senator Glenn's Shuttle Flight." *The Chronicle of Higher Education*, April 17, 1998, pp. 20A- 21A.

Lemonick, Michael D. "Three Terrifying Minutes? Challenger's Crew May Not Have Died Instantly." *Time*, August 11, 1986, p. 55.

Leopold, George. "Navy Spy Satellite Comes in from the Cold." *Electronic Engineering Times*, June 29, 1998, pp. 1, 22.

Life Magazine. "A Bird for Outer Space." Winter 1978, p. 7.

Lovell, Jim, and Jeffrey Kluger. *Apollo 13* (previously titled *Moon Shot: The Perilous Voyage of Apollo 13*). New York: Simon and Schuster, 1994.

Lyttle, Jeff. "John Glenn: An American Story." *Columbus Monthly*, August 1998, pp. 28–34.

Murray, Charles, and Catherine Bly Cox. *Apollo: The Race to the Moon.* New York: Simon and Schuster, 1989.

NASA. "Lunar Prospector Finds Evidence of Ice at Moon's Poles." NASA Release 98–38 (http://lunar.arc.nasa.gov). March 5, 1998.

⸺. "Project Apollo." Online (http://www.hq.nasa.gov/office/pao/History/apollo.html). Washington, DC: NASA, 1993.

⸺. "Project Gemini." Online (http://www.ksc.nasa.gov/history/gemini/gemini.html). Washington, DC: NASA, 1993.

⸺. "Project Mercury." Online (http://www.ksc.nasa.gov/history/mercury/mercury.html). Washington, DC: NASA, 1993.

⸺. *Space Shuttle Mission Chronology.* NASA Kennedy Space Center Release No. 12–92. Washington, DC: NASA, January, 1995.

NASA 25 Years: The Greatest Show in Space. Videocassette. 10 vols. Madacy Entertainment Group, 1995.

Newhouse, John. *War and Peace in the Nuclear Age.* New York: Knopf, 1989.

New York Times. "Tentative Flight Plan Is Drafted for Shuttle." April 15, 1986, p. C3.

————. "Voyage of the Spaceship Columbia: An Overview of the Shuttle's Maiden Flight," April 7, 1981, p. C3.

Nixon, Richard. *RN: The Memoirs of Richard Nixon.* 2 vols. New York: Grossett and Dunlap, 1979.

Oberg, James E. *Red Star in Orbit.* New York: Random House, 1981.

Pach, Chester Jr., and Elmo Richardson. *The Presidency of Dwight D. Eisenhower.* Lawrence: University Press of Kansas, 1991.

"NASA Dumping Projects to Send Astronauts to Mars, Moon." *Peekskill Star,* January 25, 1998, p. 6B.

Powers, Robert M. *The World's First Spaceship: Shuttle.* New York: Warner Books, 1980.

Reagan, Ronald. *Speaking My Mind: Selected Speeches.* New York: Simon and Schuster, 1989.

Riskind, Jonathan. "Clinton's Visit to NASA Site Lightens Up Glenn's Training." *The Columbus Dispatch,* April 15, 1998, p. 3A.

Schieffer, Bob, and Gary Paul Gates. *The Acting President.* New York: E.P. Dutton, 1989.

Shepard, Alan B. Jr., and Deke Slayton. *Moon Shot: The Inside Story of America's Race to the Moon.* Atlanta: Turner, 1994.

————. "The First American." In M. Scott Carpenter et al., *We Seven,* pp. 173–199. New York: Simon and Schuster, 1962.

Slagle, Alton. "NASA's 'Russian Roulette.'" *New York Daily News,* June 10, 1986, p. 5.

————. "Prober Blasts Off in Attack on NASA." *New York Daily News,* February 28, 1986.

Slayton, Donald K. "A Job For Everybody." In M. Scott Carpenter et al., *We Seven,* pp. 75–83. New York: Simon and Schuster, 1962.

Sorenson, Theodore C. *Kennedy.* New York: Harper and Row, 1965.

Swenson, Loyd Jr., James M. Grimwood, and Charles C. Alexander. *This New Ocean: A History of Project Mercury.* NASA Special Publication 4201 (http://www.hq.nasa.gov/office/pao/History/SP-4201/toc.htm) Washington, DC: NASA, 1989.

Wicker, Tom. *One of Us.* New York: Random House, 1991.

Wilford, John Noble. "From the Ground Up: Space Program Faces Hurdles Despite Cheers for Columbia." *New York Times,* April 19, 1981, p. 1E.

Williams, Walter C., Kenneth S. Kleinknecht, William M. Bland Jr., and James E. Bost. *Mercury Project Summary.* NASA Publication SP-45 (http://www.ksc.nasa.gov/history/mercury/mercury.html). Washington, DC: NASA, 1963.

Wolfert, Ira. "1969: The Year of the Moon." *Reader's Digest,* May 1969, pp. 55–59.

Zornio, Mary C. "Detailed Biographies of Apollo I Crew." Online (http://www.hq.nasa.gov/office/pao/History/Apollo204/zorn/intro.htm). Washington, DC: NASA 1993.

Index

About the Author

A member of the literature and communications faculty of Pace University in Pleasantville, New York, Patrick Walsh grew up with the space program in the 1960s. Graced by his parents and brother with a love of history, he learned how to tell a story at an early age by listening to his grandfather's tales of how America changed during the twentieth century.

As an adult, the author has put those skills to use daily, publishing articles on subjects ranging from history and politics to music, theater, and popular culture.